•Bartholomew•

WALK THE ISLE OF WIGHT

by David Perrott and Laurence Main

GW00420198

Bartholomew

A Division of HarperCollins*Publishers*

CONTENTS

British Library Cataloguing in Publication Data
Perrott, David
  Walk the Isle of Wight.
  1.Isle of Wight – Visitors' guides
  I. Title   II. Main, Laurence
  914.22804859
  ISBN 0–7028–1279–X

Published by Bartholomew,
a Division of HarperCollins Publishers,
Duncan Street, Edinburgh EH9 1TA

First Published 1991
© Bartholomew 1991

ISBN 0 7028 1279 X

Printed in Great Britain by Bartholomew,
HarperCollins Manufacturing, Edinburgh

Produced for Bartholomew by
Perrott Cartographics, Darowen, Machynlleth, Montgomeryshire.
Typesetting by Perrott Cartographics and Litho Link.
Litho origination by Litho Link, Welshpool, Montgomeryshire.

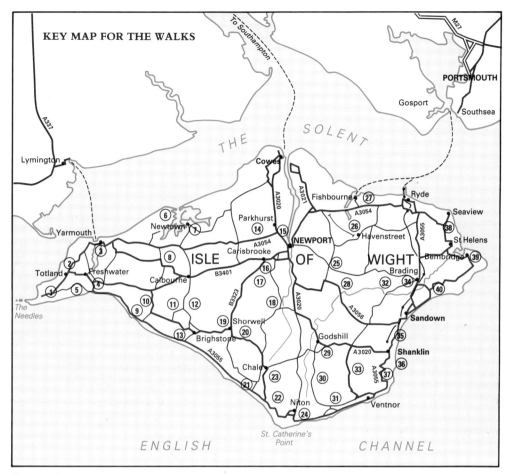

Key to the maps

Scale 1:25000

All the maps are drawn on a north axis, ie. with north at the top

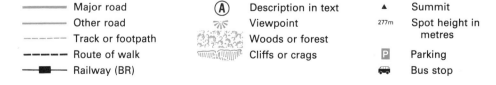

	Major road	(A)	Description in text	▲	Summit
	Other road		Viewpoint	277m	Spot height in metres
	Track or footpath		Woods or forest		
	Route of walk		Cliffs or crags	P	Parking
	Railway (BR)			🚌	Bus stop

WALKING IN THE ISLE OF WIGHT

Catamaran, hovercraft, hydrofoil and car ferry have brought the Isle of Wight to within easy travelling distance of the big cities and population centres of southern England. In spite of this it has remained an enchanting island, especially for those who explore it on foot using the ancient paths. Its scenery is splendid, and has inspired many poets who have lived within its influence. Alfred, Lord Tennyson, was the most famous, but John Keats came too, and Algernon Swinburne spent his childhood here. Novelists who have come to the island have included Charles Dickens and J B Priestley. They have expressed what everybody visiting the island soon feels: that it is vibrant, alive and offers a refreshing taste of freedom.

Isolation by the sea seems to have protected the inhabitants from the treadmill of mainland existence. The sea also adds variety to so many panoramic views and gives 60 miles (97 km) of coastline that is within sight of a considerable part of the island. Measuring roughly 23 miles (37 km) by 13 miles (21 km) (about 147 square miles or 38,000 hectares), the island is home to 130,000 inhabitants. What is surprising is how uncrowded it can seem, in spite of the million or so visitors who come each year. This is due in large part to the magnificent and varied countryside, which you can't fully appreciate from behind the window of a car or a bus. You have to get out and walk. In whichever direction you go, you won't be disappointed.

There are bare windswept downs, saltmarshes, bluebell woods, a semi-tropical jungle in The Undercliff, a variety of rock formations and, perhaps, the most cared for footpaths in the whole of England. There are about 500 miles of rights of way on the island and the County Council takes its responsibilities as the Highway Authority seriously. Can anywhere else claim such a lack of illegal obstructions?

Access is made easy for locals and visitors alike by excellent public transport, with cheap rover tickets on the local buses. If ever there was a case for visitors leaving their cars at home, it is the ferry to the Isle of Wight. Why congest the island's quiet lanes when you can travel swiftly across the Solent as a foot passenger and then enjoy riding all the buses and British Rail trains on the island for a bargain fare (especially if you buy a ticket to last a week or a month)? Not only will you not have to park a car, but you'll also gain a discount on admission to many attractions. The island caters well for its tourists and you'll find plenty to do on a rare rainy day (Shanklin and Sandown usually top the national sunshine league). With a wide choice of places to stay, you'll be made to feel welcome.

1 SAFETY AND EQUIPMENT

There are no mountains on the Isle of Wight, although you feel as though you've climbed one when on St. Boniface Down, the highest spot on the island at 787 feet (240 m). The views are superb and, of course, the height above sea level can be seen as actually being that when you are surrounded by water.

Nevertheless, you won't need to worry about emergency survival bags or even walking boots. Sensible shoes will do on all of these walks, although money spent on a good pair of walking boots and an anorak is never wasted. A rucksack and the various other items of outdoor gear can also contribute to your comfort. In summer, all you might need are a pair of shorts and a sunhat. Food and drink for a picnic always make a ramble more enjoyable, but on this island there is usually a shop, a pub or a café not far away. All walkers are advised to carry a 1:25,000 scale map and to learn how to use it, together with a good compass, although the Isle of Wight is the last place where anybody is likely to get lost.

Many of the walks in this book include coastal sections, sometimes along cliff-top paths, some of which are visibly crumbling away. Take extra care, stay away from the edge, avoid misty conditions and keep alert, especially with children.

Allow plenty of time for each route. There are often historic sites to visit, which will add to your enjoyment. Note that where approximate distances are given in the walk directions, the metric equivalents are also approximate; for example 100 yards or 90 metres.

2 RIGHTS OF WAY

All the routes in this guide follow established rights of way. Keep to the paths, which are nearly all signposted and waymarked. Many of the signs even state the path number and its destination. The route directions in this book give such information where necessary, so you should have no difficulty finding your way. If you find a stile missing or a path obstructed by crops, do inform the County Surveyor, Isle of Wight County Council, Newport, Isle of Wight who will appreciate such help. Some parishes display a 1:10000 scale map of their rights of way, perhaps in the church porch or outside the village hall.

There is a lot of National Trust land on the island. Please do remember that farmers have grazing rights over it.

If you have a dog, please ensure that it doesn't foul the public footpath, and keep it on a lead. The Animals Act (1971) states that dogs endangering livestock may be shot. The Protection of Livestock Act (1953) makes it an offence to permit a dog to worry livestock, with a maximum penalty of £200. Worrying includes being at large in a field in which there are sheep. Dogs are not usually allowed on family beaches during the summer months.

Always regard it as a privilege as well as a right to follow a right of way across someone else's land; in that way we can build an atmosphere of co-operation, rather than confrontation, in the countryside. Further information on rights of way is available from the Ramblers' Association, 1 - 5 Wandsworth Road, London, SW8 2LJ.

3 THE COUNTRY CODE

Enjoy the countryside and respect its life and work.
Guard against all risk of fire.
Leave all gates as you find them.
Keep your dogs under close control.
Keep to public paths across farmland.
Use gates and stiles to cross fences, hedges and walls.
Leave livestock, crops and machinery alone.
Take your litter home.
Help to keep all water clean.
Protect wildlife, plants and trees.
Take special care on country roads.
Make no unnecessary noise.

4 HISTORY

Prehistoric man lived on the Isle of Wight and ancient barrows are visible from several of these tracks, which are comparable with the ancient chalk ridgeways of Wiltshire, near Avebury or Stonehenge. The island was physically part of Wessex until comparatively recently – perhaps around 4000 BC. The Solent may have been fordable much later than that. Old Stone Age tools dating back to about 80,000 BC have been found on the island. Perhaps its isolation by the Iron Age explains the lack of hillforts, which are a feature of mainland Wessex.

In AD 43 the Romans called the island Vectis. Villas were built and the one near Brading now provides us with examples of excellent mosaics. These villas were used for more basic, practical, purposes by the Britons, who regained their independence from the Romans in AD 410, before they, in turn, lost possession of the island to Saxon invaders in 530. Jutes, from what is now Denmark, then seemed to settle here, while no doubt some of the Britons remained. Christianity appears to have come late to the island, in 685. The island's agricultural prosperity later attracted the Norsemen, who raided the English coast. The island's vulnerability and its strategic position from which to launch an attack on the mainland has been a constant worry ever since King Harold, the last Saxon king of England, made his main camp here in 1066, in anticipation of William of Normandy's invasion. Between 1267 and 1293 the great castle at Carisbrooke was strengthened by a young widow, the Countess Isabella. She was effectively Queen of the island. The English Crown resumed control in the 14th century, after the French ruined the town of Newport in 1377. The French continued to raid until 1404, demonstrating a desperate need for coastal defences on the island. The strong Tudor government provided these, and soon a chain of forts protected the Solent. The 'Back of the Wight', or southern coast, was less vulnerable due to its high cliffs and dangerous rocks. Local militia were raised and beacons maintained for communication. The Spanish Armada passed by, as did the English Civil War, except for King Charles I fleeing here to imprisonment at Carisbrooke Castle in 1647.

Large houses such as Appuldurcombe House were built at a time when the wealth of most of the population was based on smuggling. The island was notorious for its cheap spirits during the 17th and 18th centuries, brought in by night up some remote chine (ravine). Whole communities were involved, with some places full of farmers who sowed no crops or fishermen who never fished, but lounged around all day with pockets full of cash. The village would collect the money to sail a boat to Cherbourg and return with the goods, as Rudyard Kipling was to write: 'Brandy for the Parson, Baccy for the Clerk; Laces for a lady'. The revenue men were outnumbered and had to be eternally vigilant. Often they accepted bribes, and the smugglers always had the initiative. One smuggler, who built himself a fine house with an expensive library, bribed juries not to convict him if caught. He was said to have amassed a fortune of £40,000, and was finally imprisoned when the law was changed to make it necessary to draw jurors' names out of a hat.

When the duties on brandy, silk and tobacco were reduced early in the 19th century, the first tourists began to arrive. New coastal forts were built as a result of Palmerston's fear of a French invasion, and troops were barracked here. Lifeboat stations were also built and some of the locals turned from being successful smugglers to valiant lifeboatmen. The island's coast has seen many shipwrecks, with some described on relevant coastal walks.

Respectability came when Queen Victoria fell in love with the island as a child, and had Osborne House, near Cowes, built for her in 1846. Prince Albert had a considerable involvement in its design. Public footpaths are lacking in this area and you won't find it on the route of a walk, but it is worth a special visit. Similarly, go to see the yachts, and the Royal Yacht Squadron cannons, taken from William IV's yacht *Royal Adelaide*, at Cowes, the island's sailing Mecca.

5 GEOLOGY

The Geology Museum at Sandown is an excellent place to visit between walks. Here you will learn much of interest about the composition of the island and why so many dinosaur bones have been found here. For a small area, the Isle of Wight displays a wide variety of rock forms. These underlying rocks have a great influence on the surface vegetation and land use, and are what makes the countryside so varied and attractive. All of the rocks are sedimentary, laid down in beds under water. The oldest date back 120 million years and are part of the Wealden Group. These are a rich source of dinosaur bones, which are found on the rapidly eroding cliffs. The clay soils are given over to pasture. The next layer is Greensand, which forms high cliffs and rolling countryside. Gault clay with Upper Greensand on top of it is responsible for the spectacular landslips around the south-east coast. A chalk ridge forms the spine of the island, from the Needles in the west to Culver Cliff in the east. This ridge forms excellent walking routes. About 30 million years ago, a succession of clays and sands were deposited on the northern half of the island, making it low and gentle. Its heavy soils form meadows. Exposed rocks can be seen on the sides of chines, or deep ravines on the coast, formed by a combination of down-cutting by a stream and rapid erosion by the sea.

6 WILDLIFE

The variety of scenery offers many different types of habitat and, as a result, the Isle of Wight is a virtual microcosm of the whole of the south-east of England.

The natural climax vegetation is deciduous woodland, now extinct due to 6000 years of clearing the land for farming. Most damaging was the felling of hearts of oak for Nelson's navy. The Forestry Commission, which was formed in 1919, planted quick-growing conifer trees. Fortunately, they kept some diversity, including a new forest planted at Brighstone, which is now mostly beech. Red squirrels live in the woods, surviving here whilst the grey squirrel overruns the mainland. You could well see a fox on a walk, and badgers are also common. Many rabbits live on the downs. Woodmice, dormice, field and bank voles, water voles, stoats, weasels, moles, hedgehogs and pygmy shrews are also here, if too shy to be seen. Otters live by the larger north-flowing rivers. Slow-worms, other lizards and grass snakes may be seen, and you should look out for adders (shy creatures which move away and hide if disturbed).

Many types of tiny flowers, such as wild thyme, eyebright and salad burnet can be found on the downs. These attract butterflies, including the Adonis blue and the dark green fritillary. Grasshoppers abound. Some of the richest habitats are the chines, which are too steep for a plough. Freshwater marshes support dragonflies, and the tidal estuaries attract a wide variety of birdlife, including snipe, teal, common, little and sandwich terns, black headed and herring gulls, and oystercatchers.

7 PUBLIC TRANSPORT

If you are visiting the Isle of Wight from the mainland, crossing the Solent is part of the fun. Trains serve the departure ports of Southampton, Lymington, Portsmouth and Southsea from all parts of Great Britain, including an over-night sleeping car service from Edinburgh to Southampton. There are regular ferry services to Cowes, Yarmouth, Fishbourne and Ryde (from where there are trains to Sandown and Shanklin). Journey times vary from 8 minutes by hovercraft to one hour by car ferry. Whatever your particular requirements, your local travel agent will be able to supply exact details of operators, prices and timetables.

Although there are car ferries, why not take the opportunity to let someone else do the driving and leave your car at home? Once on the island you can obtain a Southern Vectis Road/Rail Rover Ticket. These can be bought for an evening, a day, a week or for four weeks and offer excellent value (the four weeks ticket must be bought at a Southern Vectis travel office, the others can be bought on your first bus). A comprehensive timetable, which includes the British Rail Island Line (on which your rover ticket is also valid) is available. There is a discount scheme in conjunction with the rover ticket, offering cheaper admission to places such as Arreton Manor,

Brading Roman Villa and Robin Hill Country Park. Write for full details to: The Southern Vectis Omnibus Co Ltd, Head Office, Nelson Road, Newport, Isle of Wight, PO30 1RD. Tel: (0983) 522456. As bus routes are liable to change, all services should be checked from a current timetable.

8 USEFUL ADDRESSES

The relevant Weathercall telephone forecast is on (0898) 500403.

Tourist information is available from:
The Isle of Wight Tourist Office
Quay Store, Town Quay, Newport, Isle of Wight, P030 2EF. Tel: (0983) 524343.
There are **Tourist Information Centres** at:
The Esplanade, Sandown. Tel: (0983) 403886.
67 High Street, Shanklin. Tel: (0983) 862942.
Western Esplanade, Ryde. Tel: (0983) 62905.
These remain open all year.
Seasonal **Tourist Information Centres** are open at:
34 High Street, Ventnor. Tel: (0983) 853625.
Quay Road, Yarmouth. Tel: (0983) 760015.
Fountain Yard, West Cowes. Tel: (0983) 291914.
Bus Station Car Park, Church Litten, Newport. Tel: (0983) 525450.
They all provide information on accommodation, events, attractions and entertainments.

There is an active local group of the Ramblers' Association on the Isle of Wight. Visitors are most welcome on their regular walks. Further details are available from Mrs C.R. Johns, 19 Manor Road, Lake, Sandown, Isle of Wight, PO36 9JA. Tel: (0983) 406949.

9 EVENTS

The Round the Island Yacht Race (starting and finishing at Cowes) is the largest yacht race in the world. It is usually held on the first Saturday in June. Tel: (0983) 296621 for exact details.

Cowes Week, the famous highlight of the yachting year, is held in the first week of August every year. The festivities and yacht racing culminate in a grand ball at Northwood House and a firework display over the harbour.

Every fourth year in September (next in 1993) the Round the World Race for maxi-yachts starts from Portsmouth and goes through the Solent.

THE NEEDLES
5 miles (8 km) Moderate

This is a walk full of contrasts. There is spectacular scenery, ranging from the multi-coloured cliffs of Alum Bay to the jagged rocks of The Needles. There are also fine coastal views from the heather moorland of Headon Warren and the grassy West High Down. Man has created extra points of interest, from defensive batteries overlooking the Solent to the chair-lift up to the Pleasure Park.

A The Alum Bay Glass company is worth a visit. You can watch coloured decorative and functional glassware and jewellery being made by hand, then select a gift from the showroom. Open Easter - Oct daily 10am - 5pm (no glassmaking on Sats), Oct - Thur before Easter Mon - Fri 10am - 1pm & 2pm - 5pm.

B The threat of a French invasion in the time of Napoleon III led to the Needles Old Battery being built between 1861 and 1863 on the instructions of Lord Palmerston. This stood on a promontory 250 feet (75 m) above the sea. It was defended inland by a dry ditch crossed by a rolling bridge. The advent of torpedo boats in the 1880s led to experiments with searchlights and quick-firing guns to find them and stop them. As a result an armoured searchlight emplacement was built between 1898 and 1899 at the most westerly point of the island. The tunnel connecting it to the battery parade ground now gives access to the closest land view of The Needles. These rocks are composed of chalk and have been considerably eroded over the years. The slim 120 feet (35 m) pinnacle which gave The Needles their name crashed into the sea in 1764. Ships have also been wrecked here, including the *Irex*, on 25th Jan 1890. Bound for Rio de Janeiro from Greenock with a cargo of iron pipes, she had turned up the Channel for safety. She was the biggest sailing ship (2347 tons) ever to become a total wreck on the island's shores. Of the 36 aboard, 29 were saved thanks to a line secured by a record-breaking rocket launch and the extraordinary bravery of coastguards, soldiers and local people. The red light of The Needles Lighthouse, which was built in 1859 and stands 109 feet (33 m) high, had been seen by the captain of the *Irex*, who imagined it to be the bright light of a pilot boat.

In 1903 the obsolete guns of the battery were thrown over the cliff, and the New Needles Battery was built on more stable chalk higher up. The Old Battery was used as a testground for Britain's first anti-aircraft (AA) gun in 1913 and the AA guns placed here during World War II were the first to be fired from the battery in anger. The headland was bought by the National Trust in 1975, restored and officially opened by the Prince of Wales in 1982. Open Easter, and Jun - Sept daily 10.30am - 5pm. Apr, May, Oct - Dec Sun - Thur 10.30am - 3.30pm. Admission charge.

C The New Needles Battery was built between 1893 and 1895. The engine for the *Black Knight* space rocket was tested near here between 1956 and 1971.

D Headon Warren is owned by the National Trust and provides fine views across the Solent. This sandy heath is a popular picnic spot and was once the location of Hatherwood Point Battery. Built between 1865 and 1869, this was the control point for all the guns defending the ship channel during the searchlight experiments of 1889-92. Soil erosion caused the site to be abandoned by 1900.

E Alum Bay was given its name because alum ore was once mined here. Now its wealth is derived from the 12 or more different shades of sand which compose its crumbling cliffs. Come after rain for the best view and buy, if you wish, a souvenir filled with the coloured sands. You can also take a boat trip from here during the summer for a really close view of The Needles.

F The Needles Pleasure Park can come as a shock to the system after a peaceful country ramble. Perhaps that's why you should consider using the chair-lift to reach it from the beach.

Over

0   1 mile

0   1 km

6 *Veer slightly right along path T21 signposted to Alum Bay. Bear left at a path junction. Then keep to the perimeter path around Headon Hill, ignoring a fork on the left. Reach a Coastal Path waymark post and veer left to descend to Alum Bay. Turn sharply left down a track to a gate at the foot of Headon Warren. Go through and turn right to pass the entrance to the Alum Bay Tearooms on your right and descend to the beach at Alum Bay.*

5 *You reach a gate and stile on your left with a gateway opposite. Turn left over the stile. Walk with a fence on your right to a stile in the top fence. Go ahead to the B3322 road, cross it and take the signposted path T20 opposite, crossing a stile beside a gate. This hedged path bears left to another stile. Go over this onto Headon Warren, following the hedged path to a signpost.*

7 *Bear left under the chair-lift to admire the multi-coloured cliffs.* **Either** *ride on the chair-lift up to the Needles Pleasure Park or retrace your steps to where a staircase on your right leads to the top station of the chair-lift. Go ahead through the Pleasure Park to the bus stop at its entrance.*

1 *Start from the bus stop at The Needles Pleasure Park, Alum Bay (buses 7, 7A & 17 from Ryde, and 42 from Yarmouth). Motorists can park nearby, at the western end of the B3322 south of Freshwater.*
With your back to the Pleasure Park, go right, soon passing the coach park on your left and the car park on your right. Follow the access lane to The Needles Old Battery.

Headon Warren

B3322

Chair Lift

Alum Bay

West High Down

Highdown Cliffs

The Needles

Needles Old Battery

Coastguard Cottages

2 *Retrace your steps 600 yards (550 m) and turn sharply right up steps to a stile. Continue climbing with the path to a stile below Coastguard Cottages (now National Trust holiday cottages). Go ahead across this to The Needles Viewpoint then retrace your steps to the stile.*

3 *Cross the stile and turn right uphill past the cottages on your right to the top of West High Down. Bear left to continue above and parallel to a fence, with the sea on your right. Eventually your path will dip to a junction marked by a half-size replica of a navigation beacon that used to stand on Tennyson Down.*

4 *Do not cross the stile beside the gate before the replica beacon. Turn sharply left along the signposted path T25. Reach an old chalk pit on your left and turn right level with it to cross a stile beside a gate. Follow a hedged path past Alum Bay Cottage on your right and continue to the B3322 road. Go right up Alum Bay Old Road.*

Walk 2
GOLDEN HILL FORT
5.5 miles (8.9 km) Easy

The west of the Isle of Wight was once of crucial strategic importance to the defence of the realm, and its coastline has been well embellished with fortifications. These now add interest to this walk as they have been rendered obsolete for military purposes. In a central position behind the coastal forts was Golden Hill Fort, now in the middle of open country.

A Golden Hill Fort was part of Lord Palmerston's response to *La Gloire*, the first warship to be armoured with iron plates, which was launched by France in 1859. Suddenly the wooden-hulled battleships of the Royal Navy were obsolete and there was fear of invasion. The key to national security was now seen to be the fortification of the major naval bases (especially Portsmouth) from which British ironclads could meet any invasion fleet. The Needles Passage had to be defended since it was the 'back door' to the Solent and the port of Southampton, as well as the large naval base of Portsmouth. The new coastal batteries also needed covering against assault from the landward side. Golden Hill Fort was to both provide that cover and to serve as a barracks for the small coastal batteries. The 1859 Royal Commission reported the need for a fort with 12 guns and 400 men at Hill Farm. The existence of yellow laburnum bushes there christened the fort Golden Hill. Trimming costs, a fort smaller than originally planned was built between 1863 and 1872. Its hexagonal defensible two-storey barrack was designed to house eight officers, 128 of other ranks plus 14 hospital patients. They were to be defended by 18 roof-top guns, but only six were installed. These were removed in 1903. Guns and ammunition were stored here, however, and the fort became the Western District School of Gunnery from 1888 until 1940. The survivors from the Royal Militia of Jersey (known as the 11th Battalion of the Royal Hampshire Regiment) then made it their home, as did Canadian soldiers. Water transport units of the Royal Army Transport Corps took the place over as their barracks in 1945 but the Army moved out in 1962, selling the fort in 1964. An industrial estate existed here between 1969 and 1984 but the fort was then restored and opened to visitors in 1985. Amid the craft shops, doll museum and camera museum there is a military museum and a Sir Winston Churchill Room containing memorabilia of the great man.

B Colwell slipway was used to unload heavy guns for the many forts in West Wight.

C Fort Albert stands four-square in the sea off Cliff End, the next headland as you walk north along the sea wall from the pier at Totland. Named after Prince Albert, who took a keen interest in its construction, the fort was completed in 1856, with accommodation for 300 men. In the early 1880s its design became outdated. The mounted guns were removed and it became an infantry barracks. It later found a new lease of life as a launching station for the experimental Brennan torpedo from 1886 to 1888. The fort is now a block of luxury flats and there is no public access.

D The entrance to Fort Victoria Country Park is beside Cliff End Battery, on your left. A three-gun earthen battery was thrown up against the threat of Napoleon in 1798. By 1858 a guardhouse, ditch and palisade mounted by 11 guns were overlooking the new Fort Albert, protecting it from musket fire from the slopes.

E Fort Victoria dates back to 1853 and is the third fort to be built on this site since 1547. Its triangular shape was reputedly designed by Prince Albert. Built on top of the old Sconce Point Battery, its seaward walls are set at right angles to each other with space for 10 guns in casements in each. Obsolete by 1859, the building was used by the Royal Artillery as a barracks. The Royal Engineers (who were responsible for laying minefields in coastal waters) took it over in 1891 and helped to rescue 223 of the crew of the wrecked cruiser *Gladiator* in 1908. The fort now houses a museum and a café.

Over

0   1 mile

0   1 km

5 *Bend left with the fenced path, then bear right into Fort Victoria Country Park. Follow the main path through woodland until a sign points left to Fort Victoria and its café. Turn left along the woodland path to it. Pass the fort on your left and take the access lane ahead.*

6 *Follow the lane as it bends right, ignoring the signposted Coastal Footpath to Yarmouth on your left. Take the third turning on your right (signposted path F3 to Colwell). This is also Linstone Drive.*

4 *Turn left up the access lane to Bramble Farm (signposted path F10). Pass this farm on your left and go ahead along a narrow path signposted Coastal Footpath F9. It soon bends right, then left, into Linstone Chine Holiday Park. Reach a signpost and go right to Monks Lane. Turn left to follow the lane almost to its end, then turn right over a stile along the signposted Coastal Footpath F6.*

7 *When the road bends right, bear left along the signposted path. Go over a stile beside a gate to follow a hedge on your right up a long field. Continue past woodland on your right then veer left to follow the hedge on your left. Ignore a track on your left but cross a stile on your left just after it and turn right to walk with a fence on your right to a stile giving access to Monks Lane. Go left to the A3054 and left again for the signposted access on the right to Golden Hill Fort.*

1 *Start from the car park at Golden Hill Fort. This is signposted south of the A3054, on your left as you drive from Yarmouth to Freshwater. Drive all the way up the access lane to the fort to find the car park on your right. If you come by bus take nos 7, 7A & 17 from Ryde, or 42 from Yarmouth and alight on the A3054 near the signposted access lane to Golden Hill Fort, and close to where a road forks off to Norton Green.*

Walk towards the entrance tunnel to the fort, but bear right just before it to follow a waymarked bridlepath. Ignore a path on your left and go down to a signpost. Turn right along path F16 to reach Sunset Close. Go right along the pavement to Avenue Road.

3 *Turn right along the sea wall to walk with Totland Bay on your left. Reach the slipway at Colwell Chine and turn right up Colwell Chine Road. Reach the A3054 at Colwell Bay Inn and turn left along its pavement.*

2 *Go ahead at the crossroads along The Avenue to reach Colwell Road. Turn left into Totland. Pass The Mall on your left and immediately turn right along path T2 to Totland Bay. Descend steps to reach the pier.*

Fort Victoria

Norton

Fort Albert

Colwell Bay

Monks Lane

Colwell

Golden Hill Fort

Warden Point

Totland Bay

Freshwater

Pier

Totland

11

Walk 3
THE YAR ESTUARY
4.5 miles (7.2 km) Easy

The River Yar was once a tributary of a 'River Solent', with its source far to the south. It was a much larger river in the times before land and sea levels changed, but all that now remains of its former stature is an over-size estuary. This has now silted up to produce marshes and mudflats which are good feeding grounds for a wide range of birds. Come here to see grey heron, cormorant, curlew, coot, moorhen, redshank, blackheaded gull, lapwing, dunlin, ringed plover, mute swan and teal.

A Yarmouth was attacked and burnt by the French in 1377 and 1524. The threat of another French attack led King Henry VIII to construct a low, square-shaped castle here in 1547. It included the earliest known English example of an arrow-head bastion. This sharp shape enabled the guns to defend all the walls of the castle, which was built to provide a firm platform for cannon whilst presenting no target for enemy fire. The builders may either have used stone from a dissolved monastery, or from a church that stood on this site until it was ruined in a French attack. This is suggested by the sculpted hand in the floor of the long room. The Tudors were known to have had 12 cannons in the castle, of which eight were probably on the platform. The gun tracks indicate that the Victorians had four guns on the platform. The entrance to the castle was defended by a moat, portcullis and door, all to be lost when Sir Robert Holmes, appointed Captain of the island in 1669, demolished earthworks, filled in the moat and built a house (now the George Hotel) which blocked the original, eastern, entrance. The magazine was in the bottom corner of the castle, furthest from enemy fire, although the fireplaces found in the inner magazine room suggest that it was originally the gunners' living quarters. They later lived in the garrets. This move indicates the change in function from defence to garrison. Despite its guns being renewed in 1855, the castle was abandoned in 1885, and was subsequently used by the coastguard. Now in the care of English Heritage, it is open Apr - Sept daily 10am - 6pm. Admission charge.

B This tidal mill was built in 1793 and its direct access for ships led to corn being exported from here to the mainland. Sea beet (native spinach), wild parsnip (do not touch this – it can irritate the skin) and wild carrot can be seen nearby on the sea wall.

C The Freshwater, Yarmouth and Newport Railway, opened in 1889, was intended to link with a mainland route to Southampton. It shut in 1953 and its old trackbed is now lined with hawthorn. The pale pink flowered marsh-mallow plants can also be seen, as can typical salt-marsh plants.

D All Saints Church, Freshwater, is a Saxon foundation with an old, and quite extensive, graveyard. It contains the grave of Emily, Lady Tennyson, the wife of Alfred Lord Tennyson (the poet is buried in Westminster Abbey). It can be found by the east wall of the churchyard, overlooking the River Yar. Born in 1813, Emily married Alfred in 1850 after a long wait caused by the poet's lack of funds. Alfred became poet laureate to Queen Victoria – in succession to William Wordsworth – and saw the publication of his popular *In Memoriam AHH* in 1850. 'AHH' was Tennyson's dead friend, Arthur Hallam, who had been engaged to Alfred's sister, also called Emily. When the poet married Emily Sellwood at Shiplake-on-Thames, he said 'The peace of God came into my life'. Their first son was stillborn in 1851, but their second son was born in 1852 and named Hallam. A third son, Lionel, was born in 1854, the year in which *The Charge of the Light Brigade* was written. They were now wealthy and living on the Isle of Wight. This became their parish church and when G F Watts designed a window on its south side, he used Emily Tennyson as a model for the angel on the top right. One of Alfred's sisters, Mathilda, lived to the age of 98 and is buried near Emily, who died in 1896, four years after her husband.

Over

0   1 mile

0   1 km

1 *Start from the Tourist Information Centre in Yarmouth. This is near the ferry terminal (from Lymington) and the bus stops (nos 7, 7A & 17 from Ryde and 42 from Alum Bay). A car park is signposted off the A3054.*
Cross the road to visit Yarmouth Castle. Go right when leaving the castle to pass the Tourist Information Centre on your left, then the harbour on your right. Continue past the bus stops and the car park on your right, following River Road (A3054).

8 *Continue over a stile in the corner of the wood and follow the path along the edge of the wood on your left, then through the trees ahead. Emerge at a roadside signpost and go left to reach the A3054. Turn right, back to Yarmouth.*

7 *Keep to the track as it follows a hedge on your right, then bears right through a gap in the hedge and across a field to a signpost. Follow the Freshwater Way towards Yarmouth over a waymarked stile and a footbridge. Go through trees and over another footbridge and a stile, then bear left along the edge of a field to a stile. Cross it and go ahead beside a fence on your right to a wood.*

6 *Just before you reach Kings Manor Farm, turn left over two stiles marked by a signpost. Turn right immediately to follow the edge of the field to a kissing-gate. Go ahead (along the Freshwater Way) at a crosstracks, continuing over a waymarked stile beside a gate.*

2 *Turn right up Mill Road until it bends left, then go ahead along the signposted path to Freshwater. Walk with the River Yar on your right and pass a tidal mill on your left. Ignore a signposted path to Thorley on your left. Go ahead along the old sea wall with the estuary on your right.*

3 *Bear right along the line of the dismantled railway. Ignore a signposted path to Wilmington on your left. Continue along the old track-bed to The Causeway at Freshwater.*

4 *Turn right along The Causeway to reach All Saints Church, Freshwater.*

5 *Turn right up the signposted path F1 towards Yarmouth, passing the church on your right. Go ahead over a stile and walk with first the churchyard wall, then a fence on your right. Cross another stile and maintain your direction along a rough lane past bungalows on your left.*

Ferry (to Lymington)

Yarmouth Castle

A3054

A3054

P

Ⓐ

Ⓑ

Ⓒ

Saltern Wood

River Yar

Mill Copse

Kings Manor Farm

Ⓓ

Church

Backet's Copse

The Causeway

13

Walk 4
FRESHWATER BAY
4 miles (6.4 km) Moderate

Spectacular coastal scenery is complemented by interesting inland paths to produce an excellent walk with fine views. Good signposting makes route finding easy (this walk follows part of the Freshwater Way) while the beach and the café will entice you to spend a day here. The chalk downlands support a rich and varied plant life, as does the inland marsh. Look out for the natural arch near the end of the walk. This route can be linked with Walk 5.

A Afton Down has two dozen ancient barrows spread along it, culminating in a long barrow at its western end. A disc-barrow has been made into a golf-tee.

B Freshwater Redoubt, a small fortification, once guarded the bay. It is now a tea room. The cliff face below is where samphire used to be collected by men lowered down on ropes. It was then pickled and sent to London.

Freshwater Bay

Over

0   1 mile

0   1 km

4 Pass a row of terraced cottages on your left to reach Stroud Road. Bear right along the road to a crossroads and go up Hooke Hill for 20 yards (18 m). Turn right up the path signposted F38 to The Causeway. Go downstream when you reach a river. Cross a stile onto a road and turn right. Ignore path F61 (left and right) and path F25 (on your left).

3 Pass the backs of houses on your left to reach a lane at a signpost. Turn left to a crossroads and turn right up Easton Lane. Look for a signpost and stile on your right and bear right along path F37. Cross a field to a stile in a fence ahead, continue across the garden of a hotel on your left and across a stile in a hedge ahead.

A3055

The Causeway

B3399

Freshwater Bay

P

(A) Afton Down

(B)

Freshwater Bay

A3055

5 Follow The Causeway to its junction with the B3399. Go left 30 yards (27 m) then turn right up the signposted Freshwater Way to Compton (the unmetalled Manor Road). Fork left after 30 yards (27 m) up path F31. Follow this track to the foot of Afton Down.

6 Cross a stile beside a gate and take the signposted path F32 ahead. Bend right with the track to a signpost and go left along path F54 (towards Compton). Pass a golf course on your right and notice the view on your left across the island to Hampshire.

7 Bend right with the track to join a chalky path. Turn right with the sea on your left to follow the path towards Freshwater Bay. Turn left at the A3055 to the National Trust's car park at Afton Down. Turn right to cross the road and follow the Coastal Path along the cliffs to the bay. Notice the natural arch on your left and descend the steps to the bay to return to the Mermaid Café.

2 Where path F52 branches away to the right, maintain your direction along the path signposted F36 to Freshwater. Cross a stile and follow a fenced path past a field on your left to steps in a corner. Descend to take a boardwalk across a marsh.

1 Start from the Mermaid Café, by the bus stop (nos 1B, 1C, 7, 7A & 17 from Ryde) at Freshwater Bay. A car park is nearby where the A3055 makes a sharp bend. Take the signposted path F52 opposite the café towards Yarmouth (Coastguard Lane).

TENNYSON DOWN

4 miles (6.4 km) Moderate

0 _____ 1 mile

0 _____ 1 km

This is one of the finest walks on the island, and was certainly Lord Tennyson's favourite. The Poet Laureate was a familiar sight here in his black coat and broad-brimmed sombrero, enjoying the sea breezes and magnificent views of the Channel and across the island to the New Forest and Dorset. By contrast, the return path is wooded and sheltered. It passes near Farringford, Lord Tennyson's home. This route can be linked with Walk **4**.

4 *Turn sharply right along the chalk track that is signposted as path T24 to Freshwater Bay. This begins by passing a half-size replica of the old Nodes Beacon on your left. Pass an old chalk pit on your right. Go ahead along a signposted path, ignoring a track on your left.*

5 *Ignore a waymarked path on your right and go ahead into trees, following a path with a hedge on your left and trees on your right. Maintain this direction when joined by a path from your left, pass a second chalk pit on your right and veer right at a fork.*

6 *Continue across a path at a National Trust notice and emerge in a corner of a field. Walk with a hedge on your left down to a road. Visit the thatched church on your left before turning right to go back to the start.*

3 *Reach the celtic cross that is the memorial to Alfred, Lord Tennyson. Veer right away from the cliffs to converge with a chalk track at a signpost beside a gate ahead.*

2 *When the lane bends left, go ahead through a gate towards the sea.* **Take care on the cliffs!** *Bear right to walk with a fence on your right and the sea on your left along the cliff-top path. Enter the National Trust land at Watcombe Bay and keep following the cliff-top path.*

1 *Start from the bus stop at Freshwater Bay, which is served by buses 1B, 1C, 7, 7A & 17 from Ryde. There is a car park nearby at the corner of the A3055, 1 mile (1.6 km) south of Freshwater. Take the lane to Fort Redoubt signposted as path F50 (Tennyson Trail), passing public toilets on your right.*

A Freshwater Redoubt is one of the coastal fortifications built in the mid-19th century when a French invasion was feared. Queen Victoria came to tea here in 1860 with her four-year-old daughter Beatrice. You can do the same today as part of the redundant fort is open as a tea room.

B The eastern part of High Down (National Trust) was renamed after Alfred, Lord Tennyson, who lived nearby at Farringford from 1853 until 1892. The highest point, 482 feet (147 m), is now marked by a memorial cross to the poet. The views are impressive, and must have inspired much of the poetry written at Farringford, including the *Idylls of the King*. Now a hotel, Farringford was once visited by so many famous people that Anne Thackeray, daughter of the novelist, observed 'everybody at Freshwater is either a genius, or a poet, or a painter or peculiar in some way'. In 1869, Tennyson tired of the summer sightseers and found a second home in Sussex. He returned to Farringford each winter. The chalk down is also noted for its orchids.

C This is a half-size replica of the old Nodes Beacon, which once stood on the site of Tennyson's memorial cross.

D This thatched church was built in 1908 on land given by Lord Tennyson.

HAMSTEAD

6.5 miles (10.5 km) Easy

This is a fairly flat but varied walk, with plenty of water around. Western Haven is an attractive, wooded finger of the Newtown River where French ships used to sail to raid Newtown. Now it is frequented by brightly coloured yachts. The path descends to the beach to pass a memorial and a rock ledge.

5 *Reach a signpost and turn right up steps to cross a stile. Follow a path ahead to a long footbridge. Go across and veer left as waymarked to a stile in the hedge. Cross this and turn right to follow the hedge to an inlet ahead. Bear right over a stile to follow the path around the inlet on your left. Emerge over a stile into a field and walk with the hedge on your left to a stile giving access to a track. Turn right along this track back to the Coastal Footpath sign in the woods. Go left back to Shalfleet.*

4 *Ignore a signposted stile on your left. Take a track past Hamstead Farm on your right (Coastal Footpath S3). Descend to the beach, with the sea on your left. Pass the memorial on your right.*

3 *Turn right along the wide track signposted Coastal Footpath (S27) to Lower Hamstead. Cross the bridge between Ningwood Lake and Western Haven. Ignore tracks to Pigeon Coo Farm on your left. Notice when the Coastal Footpath takes a track on your right (signposted S28), **because you will return to this point**. Meanwhile go ahead to Hamstead Farm, ignoring a stile, but not the view, on your right.*

2 *Turn right up the signposted Coastal Footpath S11 to Lower Hamstead. Walk beside a hedge on your right to a footbridge, which you turn right across. Bear right along a woodland path to a signpost.*

1 *Start from the church of St. Michael the Archangel, Shalfleet, where the no 7 bus between Ryde and Freshwater stops. There is a car park nearby, up Mill Road.*
Facing the church, go right along the A3054, passing Shalfleet House.

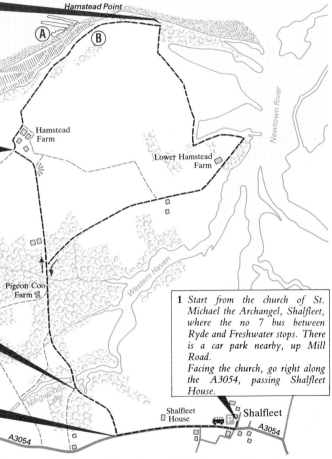

A Hamstead Ledge is an outcrop of limestone. The cliffs are of special scientific interest, being rich in fossils. Crocodile, turtle shell and shark teeth have been found here, exposed by the sea.

B This memorial to three young men lost at sea near here in the 1930s is in the form of a celtic cross.

17

NEWTOWN

2.3 miles (3.7 km) Easy

Newtown is a peaceful, out-of-the-way corner of the island, and a haven for birds. They flock to its surrounding mudflats, which are a paradise for waders, herons and gulls, and geese in winter. Butterflies such as the painted lady or the holly blue abound in summer. Yet this quiet spot was once the capital of the island. This walk takes you over the grid of a medieval 'new town' that has long vanished.

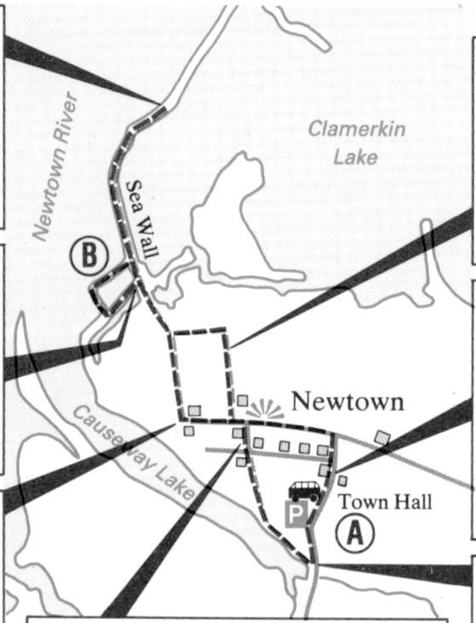

5 *Walk along the sea wall until it is obstructed, then retrace your steps to the boathouse. Turn right to walk past the old salt pans on your left, with gull island on your right. Bend left to return to your outward route.*

6 *Turn right across the long footbridge. Continue along the signposted footpath to the village, going through a kissing-gate. Walk with a hedge on your left to go through another kissing-gate in the top corner.*

7 *Go left along a hedged path to a lane. Follow this to where it bends right and take the signposted path CB14a (Gold Street) ahead. Cross the stile beside a gate at the end of this long meadow. Turn right along a lane to pass Noah's Ark on your left and return to the Old Town Hall.*

3 *Continue past the church of the Holy Spirit on your right. When the road (Church Street) bends left (into Gold Street) maintain your direction by going ahead through the gate of Marsh Farm House and following a hedged path towards the sea.*

4 *Go through a gate into a nature reserve, passing an observation post on your right. Follow the path as it bends left to a gate. Turn right to cross a long footbridge to a boathouse. Go ahead along the sea wall.*

1 *Start from the Old Town Hall, Newtown. A car park and a stop for the no 35 bus from Ryde are nearby.*
With your back to the Town Hall, go left along old Broad Street almost as far as the stone-arched Cassey Bridge.

2 *Turn right over a stile along the signposted path just before the bridge. Pass mud-flats on your left. Go ahead over a stile, and walk with a fence between you and the creek on your left. Cross a second stile ahead. Bear right to walk diagonally up a field to cross a stile in its top corner, and follow a hedged path to the old High Street.*

Map labels: Newtown River, Clamerkin Lake, Sea Wall, B, Newtown, Causeway Lake, P, Town Hall, A

A A settlement here was sacked by the Danes in 1001. The Bishop of Winchester then planned a 'new town' in the 13th century. It was based on a grid plan, following the points of the compass. The residents were released from feudal duties, explaining the town's original name of Francheville (Freetown). The importance of its harbour was recognised by the granting of a Charter to the town by King Edward II in 1318. This allowed a weekly market and an annual fair, which was known as a Randy and continued every July until 1781. Randy was derived from *rendez-vous*. The French burned the town to the ground in 1377, however, and much trade was lost to Newport and Yarmouth. Despite this, the burgesses were given the right to elect two members of parliament from 1584 until the first Reform Act in 1832. The Old Town Hall at Newtown was built in 1699, when the borough was now little more than a hamlet. The building is now in the care of the National Trust, and is open Apr - Sept Mon, Wed & Sun, plus Good Fri, Easter Sat and Tues & Thur Jul - Aug 2 - 5 pm. Admission charge.

B Sea water was evaporated in these pans to obtain salt.

Walk 8
CALBOURNE MILL
4.5 miles (7.2 km) Easy

This walk follows the Caul Bourne from Shalfleet to Calbourne Mill, which was mentioned in the Domesday Book of 1086. It is now preserved as part of an agricultural museum, where the attractive buildings house a tea room. The return to Shalfleet is by way of Dodpits Lane and Dodpits Cross. There are tales of a gallows here and the ghost of a hanged man has reputedly been seen.

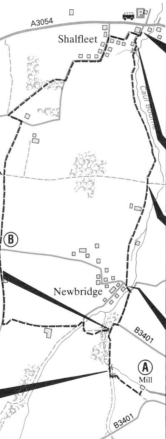

7 *Cross the dismantled railway again and reach a lane at a signpost. Go left for 150 yards (135 m) then turn sharply right along the signposted path S15 to Shalfleet. This bears right through a gap in a hedge and goes diagonally across a field to a stile in the hedge opposite. Cross the corner of the next field to a waymarked stile. Take a woodland path to a lane in the far right corner of the wood. Go left along the lane back to Shalfleet.*

6 *Go left along the path through the hedge and descend to a footbridge. Cross this and bear left then right, as waymarked, across a field. Bear left at the field edge to walk with the hedge on your right to a signpost in a corner. Turn left along path S22 to Chessell Road. When at the road, go right to its junction with the B3401. Go ahead along a track signposted S16.*

5 *Walk beside the stream on your left for 50 yards (45 m), then turn left over a brick bridge and bear right along a path which runs parallel to a stream on your left. Cross a stile in the fence ahead to reach the Water Mill and Museum of Rural Life at Calbourne. Retrace your steps to the path already noted in the hedge.*

1 *Start from the Church of St. Michael the Archangel, Shalfleet. The no 7 bus (between Ryde and Freshwater) stops outside. A car park is nearby up Mill Road. Turn right to the traffic lights on the A3054 at New Inn and turn right again up a lane which passes the church on your right. Turn left up the signposted path S17 to Newbridge.*

2 *Cross a stile, followed by a footbridge and a second stile. Continue beside a stream on your left until a waymark arrow directs you to bear right to cross the line of the dismantled railway.*

3 *Continue along the hedged track signposted S36 to Newbridge. Pass a farm on your right and take its access lane. When this turns left, go over a stile ahead. Follow the path to a stile in the hedge ahead (ignoring a stile in the fence on your right). Continue to a road.*

4 *Go left to a road junction and turn right towards Calbourne. When the road bends left, veer right over a stile beside a gate to follow the signposted path CB11 to Calbourne Mill. **Notice the path through the hedge on your right – you will take it on your return journey!** Go ahead, keeping close to the hedge on your left. Cross a footbridge over a stream ahead and go over a stile.*

A Calbourne Water Mill and Museum of Rural Life is open Easter - Oct daily 10am - 5.30pm. Admission charge. You can hand feed the tame water birds and peacocks.

B This is Dodpits Cross where one of the island's best known ghosts is supposedly seen. On some dark nights the signpost is said to change into a gibbet.

7 miles (11.3 km) Moderate

0   1 mile

0   1 km

This section of the island's coastline has cliffs composed of Wealden Marl. These have crumbled to reveal the fossilised bones of dinosaurs which walked this area over 100 million years ago. Brook Bay has been the scene of many shipwrecks, with the local lifeboat earning fame for its many courageous rescues. This route climbs the chalk down to give views of two historic houses, then returns along a woodland path.

3 *Go right along the signposted path BS86. Ignore the signposted path BS86a on the left. Although this is the route of the Hamstead Trail, it may be overgrown. Go ahead along the farm access lane to a signpost. Turn left up path BS49 to Brook Down. Ignore a fork up to a gate on your right but bend left with the track to a junction. Bear right along the hedged track signposted BS89.*

2 *Turn left up the Hamstead Trail (the signposted path BS51 to Brook Down). Follow the rough track to Dunsbury Farm, where it bends left, then right to a signpost.*

4 *Bear right close to the hedge and pass old chalk pits on your left. Go through a gate to reach a road, at which you turn right. Ignore a signposted bridle road to Newport on your left. Ignore another public footpath on your left but just after it fork left up the drive to Brook Hill House.*

5 *Fork left along the signposted path into the forest when the drive bends right towards Brook Hill House. Look for a narrow woodland path on your right and turn right down it, through the trees. Cross a stile in the perimeter fence and maintain your direction across a field.*

Dunsbury Farm

B

B3399

Hulverstone

A

A3055

Brook

C

Hanover Point

F

Brook Bay

Brook Chine

E

A3055

1 *Start from the National Trust car park at Shippards Chine and Hanover Point, on the seaward side of the A3055, 1 mile (1.6 km) west of Brook. Buses no 1B Ryde to Alum Bay and 17 Ryde to Yarmouth stop here.*
With your back to the car park, go left along the A3055 (Military Road) for 50 yards (45 m), then turn right through a gate along the signposted path 57. Ignore a signposted path on your left **opposite Compton Grange and go ahead along path BS87 towards Brook.**

D

Over

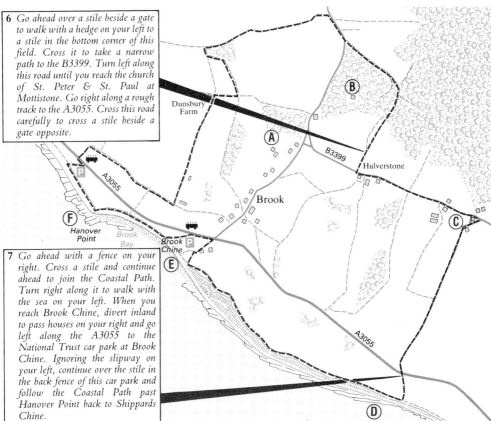

6 *Go ahead over a stile beside a gate to walk with a hedge on your left to a stile in the bottom corner of this field. Cross it to take a narrow path to the B3399. Turn left along this road until you reach the church of St. Peter & St. Paul at Mottistone. Go right along a rough track to the A3055. Cross this road carefully to cross a stile beside a gate opposite.*

7 *Go ahead with a fence on your right. Cross a stile and continue ahead to join the Coastal Path. Turn right along it to walk with the sea on your left. When you reach Brook Chine, divert inland to pass houses on your right and go left along the A3055 to the National Trust car park at Brook Chine. Ignoring the slipway on your left, continue over the stile in the back fence of this car park and follow the Coastal Path past Hanover Point back to Shippards Chine.*

A This is Brook House, where Garibaldi, the Italian patriot, planted a tree when on a visit in 1864.

B Brook Hill House is a former home of J B Priestley, the author.

C The chancel roof of the church of St. Peter & St. Paul, Mottistone, is lined with cedar boards from the wrecked Bermudan barque, *Cedrene*, stranded on Ship Ledge in 1862.

D This is where the 308 ton barque *Cedrene* was wrecked on 2nd April, 1862, in thick fog and a heavy swell. A lovely ship, just 16 days old, she had come from Bermuda with a cargo of 191 returning convicts plus 43 crew and overseers, all of whom were rescued.

E This is the old Life Boat Station at Brook. A total of 263 lives were saved by its boat between 1860 and 1936.

F The fossilised skeleton of an iguanodon was found at Hanover Point in 1972. At low tide you may see the seaweed clad stumps of a petrified forest thousands of years old.

Woodland paths lead to an ancient ridgeway, beside which the people of the Bronze Age buried their dead. From these graves you can enjoy a splendid view across the Channel. You may also see skylark and meadow pipit, joined by wheatear and ring ouzel in the spring and autumn and, in winter, stonechat. Allow time to see the creation of delicate porcelain at the Chessell Pottery.

3 Turn sharply left into the wood when you reach a track junction. Follow this woodland path as it swings right to keep to the edge of the wood on your left. Emerge through a gate in the corner of the wood.

4 Turn left through a gate to follow an uphill path beside the perimeter fence of the wood on your left. Do not take a gate into the wood, but do go ahead through two gates in the top left corner of the field. Go straight ahead to a ridgeway path.

1 Start from Chessell Pottery, which is signposted to the east at the junction of the B3401 and B3399 6 miles (9.6 km) west of Newport. Cars can be parked near the pottery. The 1C bus between Ryde and Alum Bay stops at Chessell Crossroads, from where the pottery is signposted.
Go right from the pottery to reach the B3399, bearing left along this road.

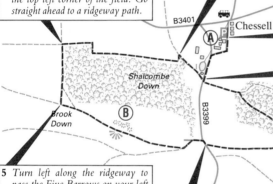

2 Turn right up the signposted path S21 towards Wellow. Bear left with this path, ignoring a path forking through a gate on your right. Walk alongside the edge of the wood on your left with a hedge on your right for 100 yards (90 m).

5 Turn left along the ridgeway to pass the Five Barrows on your left and to look over the Channel on your right. Descend with the path to pass an old chalk pit on your left. Converge with a hedge on your right before reaching a gate ahead. Go ahead to the road.

6 Cross the road to a signposted path slightly to your right. Go up it, passing tumuli in the field on your left. Go ahead through a gate into the forest. Continue 50 yards (45 m) to a cross-tracks.

7 Turn left along the forest track. Ignore a forest path on your right after 50 yards (45 m). After a further 50 yards (45 m), just before your track bends right, turn left down a forest path to join a lower path around the forest perimeter. Bear left out of the forest to a road. Turn right back to Chessell.

A Chessell Pottery is housed in a 300-year-old barn. Here you can observe all the processes in the making of exquisite porcelain. Each piece is unique, being hand-made. The designs have been inspired by nature with water gardens the central theme of the work. There is also a multitude of other flower vases and containers, table lamps, candle holders and pieces which are purely decorative. The ware is made from porcelain clay, which is a composition of china clay, feldspar and quartz. These materials produce an extremely white, hard, translucent and vitrified body. Small quantities of oxides are added to give colour. The finished product may look delicate and fragile, but the porcelain is hard and dense and travels very well.

B The Five Barrows are considered to be the best barrow group on the island. They consist of a bell-barrow, a disc-barrow and bowl-barrows (bell, disc and bowl are terms used to describe shape). Most of the barrows have been robbed and nothing is known of their original contents. The fir trees of Shalcombe Down, just to the north of the Five Barrows, cover another five bowl-barrows and a bell-barrow. A bronze knife-dagger was found in one of the bowl-barrows.

THE LONGSTONE

2 miles (3.2 km) Easy

0 ⊢————————————————⊣ 1 mile
0 ⊢————————————————⊣ 1 km

This walk takes you past one of the most mystical and magical spots on this enchanting island. The Longstone, an ancient standing stone, stands in a forest clearing, which adds to the atmosphere. The stone belongs to the New Stone Age (about 5000 years ago) when there was at the time a pattern of shifting cultivation. Extensive clearance of these chalk downs and greensand ridges was begun by the more settled Bronze Age farmers of about 3500 years ago. This century has seen the return of trees in this area, although the Corsican pine of Brighstone Forest is new to the region. This route can be combined with Walk **12**, as they both start from the same place.

3 *Cross the stile and descend between a fence on your left and trees on your right. Ignore a stile on your left in the bottom corner and turn right to walk with a fence on your left to a forest track.*

2 *Reach more tumuli on your right near a gate into the forest. Turn left here, downhill towards the sea. A clear path leads through gorse and brambles to a stile in a corner of the forest perimeter fence.*

1 *Motorists should start from the National Trust car park at Mottistone Down, which is down a lane signposted between Calbourne and Brighstone. The nearest bus stop is for the no 1B (Alum Bay to Ryde service) on the B3399 at Mottistone. Add an extra 3 miles (4.8 km) to the total distance if you are arriving by bus. Face the National Trust Information Board and turn right through a little gate beside a field gate. Walk past the gate into the forest on your right but go ahead through another small gate beside a field gate onto Mottistone Down. Walk along the old ridgeway with the forest on your right. You soon pass a round barrow on your right.*

Mottistone Down

To Brighstone

Mottistone
B3399

4 *Turn left down the forest track. Just before it bends right, look for the Longstone in a clearing on your right.*

5 *Continue the walk by crossing the stile in the fence on your left, opposite the Longstone. Go ahead around the edge of a field along a track running parallel to the forest on your right. Continue over a stile beside a gate and follow the track past woodland on your left. Cross another stile beside a gate ahead to reach Strawberry Lane.*

Turn left up it back to the car park (or go right for the nearest bus stop).

A According to an analysis of the pollen evidence, these round barrows near the pre-historic ridgeway date back to the Bronze Age (about 3500 years ago), when the chalk downs were being extensively cleared for agriculture.

B The Longstone is a free-standing upright stone of local greensand with a second stone on the ground beside it. About 13 feet (4 m) high, the Longstone seems to have belonged to a long barrow or burial mound which can be traced in the forest behind. The Longstone has most probably always stood on its own, however. The fallen stone was moved here from a site a little to the south in 1856.

C You can't see Castle Hill because it is obscured by trees, but it is an earthwork enclosure dating from the Iron Age (about 300 BC).

D This is Strawberry Lane and, yes, it does provide tiny, delicious, wild strawberries in June (and blackberries in August).

0   1 mile

0   1 km

Brighstone Forest can provide shade on a hot day, or shelter on a wet and windy one, but choose a clear day for this walk if you can, to enjoy the view from the Tennyson Trail over the village of Brighstone, once notorious for smuggling. Route finding is simple, so you can concentrate on the inspiring views and the wildlife, which includes green woodpeckers and peacock butterflies. This route can be combined with Walk **11**, as they both start from the same place.

1 *Start from the National Trust car park at Mottistone Down, which is down a lane signposted between Calbourne and Brighstone. The nearest bus stop is for the no 1B (Alum Bay to Ryde service) on the B3399 at Mottistone. Add an extra 3 miles (4.8 km) to the total distance if you are arriving by bus. Return to the road and, with your back to the car park, turn left along the road for 400 yards (360 m).*

2 *Turn sharply right through a small gate beside a large one and follow the signposted path BS9 towards Shorwell. Avoid a fork on your left near the start. Follow the broad gravel track through the forest.*

4 *Go through a little gate beside a big gate and turn right along the Tennyson Trail, ignoring a signposted stile opposite. Walk with the forest on your right and fine coastal views on your left. Reach the road and go right for the car park on your left.*

3 *Reach a signpost at a crosstracks. Turn right along the Tennyson Trail, which is path BS4 towards Brighstone.*

Brighstone Down

To Mottistone

Ⓐ   Ⓑ

Ⓒ Brighstone

B3399

A The Tennyson Trail is named after Alfred, Lord Tennyson, the poet, who lived near its south-western end and was particularly fond of walking. It is about 15 miles (24 km) long and connects Alum Bay with Carisbrooke Castle, via Tennyson Down.

B The Worsley Trail is named after an old island family. About 15 miles (24 km) long, it connects Shanklin with the Tennyson Trail here, at Brighstone Forest.

C Brighstone could claim to be the prettiest village on the island, with its thatched cottages, tea gardens and old church. The name of the pub, the Three Bishops, recalls three vicars of Brighstone who became bishops after leaving the island. They were: Bishop Ken, who wrote *Awake my soul and with the sun*; Samuel Wilberforce, whose father, William, fought to end slavery; and Dr Moberley, who was the headmaster of Winchester College before being ordained. The churchyard contains the bones of Moses Munt and Thomas Cotton, who gave their lives when trying to rescue the people trapped on board the *Sirenia* in March 1888. Previous generations had been notorious for their smuggling activities. With money to be made from salvaging wrecks, they would pray:
'Matthew, Mark, Luke and John
Bless the bed that I lie on,
Please the Lard to send a starm,
Ship ashore before the marn'!

CHILTON CHINE

2.3 miles (3.7 km) Easy

This short route includes a clifftop walk connecting two chines. These steep sided narrow gullies are formed by the dual erosion of the sea wearing away the cliff face and downward erosion by streams into the cliff. The shore below is attractive, with sand and pink-brown rock ledges revealed when the tide is out. These have provided evidence of dinosaurs living here in the past.

1 *Start from the car park on the seaward side of the A3055 at Chilton Chine, 1 mile (1.6 km) south-west of Brighstone. The no 17 bus (between Ryde and Yarmouth) stops here.*
Go right along the Military Road over a bridge. Pass the Isle of Wight Pearl company on your right and, at the end of the white wooden fence on your right, opposite a stile beside a gate across the road, turn right through a gap to follow the hedge on your left to the cliffs.

2 *Turn left along the Coastal Path to walk with the sea on your right. Pass a holiday camp on your left and reach the deep gash of Grange Chine (joined by Marsh Chine).*

3 *Turn left up the signposted path BS57 towards the Military Road (A3055). Go across it to climb over a stile and walk beside a hedge on your right along the signposted path BS61, going past Barney's Night Club on your left.*

4 *Go ahead over two stiles in the corner of a field and walk with a hedge on your right to a stile in the next field corner. Cross this and turn left to walk with the hedge on your left.*

5 *Your path switches to the other side of the hedge. Reach a lane and turn left to a sharp bend. As the lane goes right, leave it by going ahead along a signposted path to the Military Road.*

6 *Cross the road to continue down the Coastal Path at the back of the car park to reach the beach. Retrace your steps to the start of the walk.*

A The Isle of Wight Pearl company offers free admission daily 10am - 5.30pm to one of the largest single collections of pearl jewellery.

B Brighstone Holiday Camp illustrates the startling rate of erosion here. It comprised 18 acres (7 hectares) when opened in 1931. It is now down to about 7 acres (3 hectares).

C Several fine ships have been wrecked between these two chines. A tremendous south-westerly storm drove the barque *Mirabita* aground here on 5th December, 1859. She was from Malta and carried a cargo of oats from Marseilles. As the angry seas swept her to the shore her crew of 16 could be clearly seen clinging to the rigging. They couldn't be reached, however, and when her masts toppled they were thrown into the maelstrom of breaking waves below. Five survived to be pulled from the surf. The crew of the *Woodham* were luckier on 2nd February, 1873. This 640 ton Norwegian steamer was carrying a cargo of coal and soda from Newcastle to New York when her propeller shaft broke in the channel. A Liverpool steamer took her in tow, but the weather turned foul and the hawser connecting the two ships broke. They then lost contact in a dense snowstorm. The crippled ship grounded off Chilton Chine at 2 am. The lifeboat from Grange Chine managed to reach her at 7 am and brought 20 men ashore in two trips. The captain and the mate stayed on board, but eventually had to be rescued. Coxswain Buckett received the RNLI silver medal for bravery.

D Grange Chine had a grange owned by the monks of Quarr Abbey during the Middle Ages.

PARKHURST FOREST

2.5 miles (4 km) Easy

0 _____ 1 mile
0 _____ 1 km

Parkhurst Forest is a 1180 acre (478 hectares) remnant of a royal forest mentioned in the Domesday Book of 1086. In the days when wood was used for the construction of wooden sailing ships, it was a vital resource. Belonging to the Forestry Commission since 1924, the northern part has recently been replanted with oaks, with Douglas fir and Corsican pine still predominating in the southern part. Follow the walk directions carefully.

7 *Reach a waymark post and a seat on your left. Turn sharply left at a track junction to pass another seat and waymark post on your right.*

8 *Reach a corner where you turn right as waymarked along a short, grassy track to a wide gravel track.*

9 *Turn right along the gravel track. Pass a forest ride and a seat on your right.*

6 *Notice a waymark post on your left and turn right as directed by its arrow along a wide, grassy ride. Go past a seat on your left and a forest ride on your right.*

10 *When the gravel track is crossed by a grassy ride, turn right along this to a cross-tracks, where you turn left back to the gravel track.*

5 *Pass a forest ride which forks into the forest on your right. Continue along the main track for 300 yards (275 m) then bear right at a track junction.*

11 *Turn right along the gravel track to the cross-tracks met near the start of this walk, ignoring all side-tracks. Turn left to return to the car park, which is shielded by trees on the right of the track.*

4 *Pass a forest ride on your left, another on your right and then another on your left. Go ahead past another forest ride and a seat on your right.*

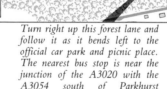

Parkhurst Forest

2 *Reach a crosstracks. Take the track on your left.*

3 *When the blue waymarked walk takes a path on your left, go ahead along the green waymarked route, passing another track and a seat on your right.*

A3054

1 *Take the A3054 west of Newport. About 1 mile (1.6 km) along the A3054, towards Yarmouth, look for a 'Parkhurst Forest Walk' sign on your right, just after two Swedish-style wooden houses.* Turn right up this forest lane and follow it as it bends left to the official car park and picnic place. The nearest bus stop is near the junction of the A3020 with the A3054 south of Parkhurst (numerous buses from nearby Newport). Step onto the lane behind the information board. Turn left to follow the green waymarks.

A Look for torn-apart cones from Scots pines at the roadside. These are evidence of red squirrels, which like to strip the pine cones scale by scale when eating them. The Isle of Wight is one of the sanctuaries for this native species, which has suffered greatly from invasion by introduced grey squirrels on the mainland. Red squirrels are shy creatures, but they do not hibernate, so you may spot one on a winter walk.

B Sweet chestnut is coppiced here. The shoots are harvested at regular intervals for fencing poles.

C Red squirrels are often seen here moving from the sweet chestnut to the Corsican pine.

MEDINA ESTUARY

4 miles (6.4 km) Easy

0   1 mile

0   1 km

Many visitors to the island change buses and shop in Newport without realising that the capital has a river with an old quay tucked away. The Medina is a popular river with amateur sailors and conservationists, in spite of the industrial development which you will have to negotiate when approaching the estuary from the town. Newport has prospered since receiving its Charter in 1190.

3 *Turn right along the signposted path N30 to the bank of the River Medina.*

2 *Go ahead along the signposted path N207. Continue over Dodnor Lane and across a long footbridge over Dodnor Creek.*

1 *Start from the bus station in Newport, the hub of the island's bus network. There is a choice of car parks nearby, all clearly signposted.*
Face Safeway's superstore and go left. Cross South Street to go up Town Lane. Continue past St. Thomas' church and Square on your left. Go ahead across High Street and up Holyrood Street. Continue ahead under a fly-over and through an industrial estate to a roundabout.

4 *Turn right to walk alongside the river on your left.*

5 *Pass Parkland Retirement Homes on your right. Do not bear right up the lane. Go ahead along the narrow riverside path signposted N30 (via Riverbank N29). Pass the Medina Valley Centre (a sailing and field study centre) and, keeping close to the river on your left, continue over a stile.*

6 *Pass Newport Rowing Club boathouse, cross a footbridge and veer right along a path between industrial units on your right and trees on your left.*

7 *Go ahead up a road, pass the quay on your left and go under a fly-over ahead. Turn left to pass the Quay Art Centre, right along Quay Street to return to the start.*

island. Passenger services between Cowes and Newport started in 1862 and finished in 1966.

C Dodnor Creek Local Nature Reserve.

D *The Ryde Queen* (the last paddle steamer from Portsmouth to Ryde). Built in 1937, she retired in 1960.

E A pirate ship which has featured on television's *Onedin Line* is moored alongside the Quay. Open Easter - Oct daily 10am - 5pm. Admission charge.

A Notice God's Providence House on the left as you enter St Thomas' Square. This is where the Plague stopped in 1584. St. Thomas' Square used to be the corn and meat market. The church at its centre was rebuilt in 1854, but it still contains the tomb of Princess Elizabeth, the daughter of King Charles I. She died of a fever at the age of 15 in 1650 whilst imprisoned, like her father before her, at Carisbrooke Castle.

B This path follows the route of the first railway line built on the

CARISBROOKE CASTLE

5 miles (8 km) Moderate, muddy after rain

This route takes you over the fertile Bowcombe Valley before climbing up to the Tennyson Trail and an inspiring ridge walk back to the start, with fine views in all directions, including the ramparts of Carisbrooke Castle. Look for the grayling butterfly, whose mottled brown adorns the chalk downs, blending with the lighter soil. The meadow path may be muddy after rain. This route can be combined with Walk **17**.

2 *Turn left over the stile before the ford to follow the signposted path N104 to Bowcombe. Walk parallel to the fence on your left to a stile ahead. Continue beside a hedge on your left and Lukely Brook on your right. Go ahead over a stile and continue to a stile and a signpost.*

6 *Maintain your direction along public bridleway 123. Descend with this to a lane and turn sharply right along it. Cross the B3323 road, go right for 20 yards (18 m) then turn left down Clatterford Shute. Retrace your steps up the signposted path N88 back to the castle.*

5 *Turn right along the Tennyson Trail at the top of the ridge, going through a gate to walk along its hedged track. Continue through a second gate, ignoring the signposted bridleway N197 on your left. Go ahead beside a hedge on your right along path N128.*

Bowcombe Down

B3341

Carisbrooke Castle

B3323

Lukely Brook

Plaish

Bowcombe

1 *Start from Carisbrooke Castle, at the end of the B3341, 1 mile (1.6 km) south-west of Newport. Bus no 5C from Ryde terminates here. With your back to the castle entrance, go left through the car park and down the signposted path N88 towards Clatterford. At the bottom of this old holloway, bear slightly right to go down Clatterford Shute (don't take Millers' Lane on your far right).*

4 *Go through a gate across your path. Turn sharply right up the signposted path N133 (to the Tennyson Trail). This path skirts the foot of the field on your left, continues through a gate and veers left to climb past an old quarry on your left.*

3 *Cross the stile and turn right along a hedged track to a junction. Go left to reach Bowcombe Farm and turn right past it to the B3323. Go right for 30 yards (27 m), then cross this road to a gate on your left. Go through it along the signposted path N132 to Bowcombe Down.*

Over

28

A 'I don't think I shall ever see a ruin to surpass Carisbrooke Castle', wrote John Keats in 1817. It is certainly set on a superb site. It may well have been occupied by Ancient Britons and Romans, but there is only sure evidence of a Saxon origin. They built a fortified camp, or burh, here to defend themselves against Viking raiders. Its stone-faced banks can still be traced on the east and west sides of the ramparts of the later Norman castle. William the Conqueror recognised the strategic importance of this site, at the heart of the island. His kinsman, William Fitzosbern, was rewarded with Carisbrooke and may have built a great hall – the one in which William the Conqueror arrested Odo, his treacherous half-brother, in 1082.

The castle came to the de Redvers family in 1100, after Fitzosbern had tried to rebel against the crown in 1078. They enlarged and improved the castle, particularly during the 'reign' of Countess Isabella de Fortibus, the tough young widow who was the last of the de Redvers line. She sold the castle to King Edward I on the day she died in 1293.

When the French raided the island in 1377, during the Hundred Years War, they destroyed Yarmouth and Francheville (now Newtown), then besieged Carisbrooke. Peter Haynoe, a bowman, went down in history as the saviour of the castle when he shot the French commander dead, having observed him making reconnaissance trips. 'Haynoe's loope', an arrow slit, can still be seen on the west side of the castle.

The threat from Spain during the 1580s led Queen Elizabeth I to appoint George Carey as governor of the Isle of Wight in 1582. He applied his distinguished political and military mind to the task and improved the island's defences. The Spanish Armada sailed past without firing a shot on 26th July, 1588, saving the castle's date with destiny for 1647, shortly after King Charles I had been defeated by the Parliamentarians. The king fled here from Hampton Court in the hope that the governor, Colonel Hammond, might help him. Although a Parliamentarian, Hammond was a nephew of the king's chaplain.

The royal guest spent his first weeks on the island in freedom, making visits, housed in comfortable rooms, attended by members of his own household and with the opportunity to escape to the continent. Cromwell would probably have preferred that he had. Unlike some of the Parliamentarians, the Protector did not hate the king and would have been relieved by his escape.

Charles was in no hurry to leave his kingdom. The prevailing uncertainties allowed him to still see some hope of a future. They also caused the fanatical Parliamentarian leaders to demand that the king be confined to the castle, have restricted access and have his bedroom door guarded at night. Hammond did his best for his monarch by turning the outer bailey into a bowling green for his recreation, but the royal prisoner soon felt the need to escape.

Farce now enters this tragic tale. Charles attempted to escape on 20th March, 1648. The king was to file through a bar in his bedroom window and escape to the curtain wall. A rope was ready to lower him from there to friends waiting with horses to take the royal party to a boat. The slim Charles declined the file, however, claiming he could squeeze through his window. In the event, he stuck at the shoulders and had to be pulled back into his room. His waiting friends dispersed, but Hammond learned of the attempt and tightened security. Three sentries were now posted to watch the king night and day. While he breathed, Charles hoped and tried again. This time, on 28th May, some nitric acid was smuggled into the king's room and was successfully used to eat through the window bars. Unfortunately, one of the bribed sentries had changed his mind and warned the governor. A scuffle led to the king's supporters fleeing empty-handed. The king was removed from Carisbrooke on 6th September and executed in London on 30th January, 1649.

Carisbrooke Castle is in the care of English Heritage, and is open daily all year 10am - 6pm (4pm Oct - Thur before Easter). Admission charge.

SNOWDROP LANE

4.3 miles (6.9 km) Moderate

Well-trodden paths provide excellent views across the centre of the island. The walk begins by following the gradual ascent of the Shepherd's Trail along an ancient ridge path. It descends only for you to turn back up Snowdrop Lane. Then there is an easy descent followed by a low-level return to the start at Carisbrooke Castle.

Allow time for a visit to this, the island's most famous monument, if you can. This route can be combined with Walk **16**.

2 *Go left to a junction and turn sharply right up the signposted path MO8 to Gatcombe. Emerge from an old holloway to walk with a hedge on your left.*

6 *Cross a stile and go right along a track. This bends left to take you to Froglands Farm. Ignore a track on your left but go ahead along the lane back to the signposted stile giving access to the narrow, hedged path on your left along which you retrace your steps back to the castle.*

5 *Follow the signposted path N202 towards Bowcombe. The track soon bends left beside a hedge on your right. Pass a track on your left, go ahead for 100 yards (90 m) and turn right along a path across the field, walking towards the castle.*

1 *Start from Carisbrooke Castle, at the end of the B3341, 1 mile south-west of Newport. There is a car park here. Bus no 5C from Ryde terminates here.*
With your back to the castle, go left from the castle entrance. Turn left through a small gate before you reach the car park and walk with the castle on your left. Go left at a corner then descend to a narrow, hedged path crossing the valley on your right. This leads to a lane.

3 *Keep beside the hedge on your left and ignore a path which forks across the field on your right. Ignore a path descending on your left. Go ahead with the hedge switching to your right. Continue past chalk cliffs on your right and through a gate ahead. Maintain your direction at a crosstracks to follow the hedge on your right down to woods. Pass a house and the Isle of Wight Hunt kennels on your left.*

4 *Turn right at the T junction along path G6 for 50 yards (45 m), then fork right up Snowdrop Lane, passing a house on your left. The metalled lane takes you to Garstons, where it is joined by a track from your right. Veer left to pass the house on your right then, ignoring the track ahead, turn right through the gate after the farm buildings.*

A Carisbrooke Castle is described in full in Walk **16**. It is best known as the place where King Charles I was kept prisoner in 1647-48. This splendid building is in the care of English Heritage and is open daily all year 10am - 6pm (4pm Oct - Thur before Easter). Admission charge.

B The distinctive tower below is part of Whitecroft Hospital.

GATCOMBE

3 miles (4.8 km) Moderate

Quiet lanes, field tracks and woodland paths take you around a remote spot near the centre of the island. The fine old church at Gatcombe is worth a visit at any time. It has stained glass windows by William Morris, and some charming associations with legend.

You may see a red squirrel in Tolt Copse.

4 Bear left at a fork, following the signposted path G6 to Chillerton. This is a metalled lane but turns into a rough track when you bear left at a junction.

3 Visit St. Olave's Church on your right before going left along the lane. Ignore a turning on your right and go ahead up a No Through Road. Pass the signposted path G8 on your right but take path G6 ahead.

5 Fork left, as waymarked, to follow the hedge on your left. Go through a gap in the corner ahead to the next field, as waymarked.

2 Turn left up the signposted path G8. Maintain your direction at a crosstracks, passing a house and a cottage on your left. Turn left along the hedged path and follow this as it bends right then left. Emerge at a gap between two fields. Turn right along a narrow, hedged path between them and continue through woodland to a lane.

6 Turn right up a track into woodland. When it bears right, veer left along the signposted path G9. Emerge at a stile, and cross it.

7 Bear left down to the bottom of this field and continue to the bottom of the next one. Turn right to walk beside a hedge on your left to a waymarked gate. Go ahead through it and continue until you notice an old quarry away to your right.

1 Start from the bus shelter opposite the school in Chillerton. This is served by bus no 16 between Newport and Ventnor. Those coming by car may park considerably in the village, which is on a minor road 2 miles (3.2 km) west of the A3020 at Rookley.
Face the school and turn right to follow the road out of the village to where it bends right.

8 Follow the track through a gate in the corner ahead. Bear left to Chillerton. Turn left along the road back to the bus shelter opposite the school.

A St. Olave's Church, Gatcombe, has many interesting features, but there is something extra here that has found expression in legend. In an alcove to the left of the altar is an effigy of a crusader, probably a member of the local Estur family. His feet rest on a little dog. This symbolic creature is said to come to life once every century or so when there is a full moon on St. John's Day (24th June). Fairies then come from the hills and woods to dance with the dog in a strange green light.

The church was built in the 13th century and the tower was added in the 15th century, probably by the same masons who worked at Carisbrooke Castle. The windows on the south side (to your right as you enter) also date from this time. Above the altar are a group of fine stained glass windows by William Morris, made when the church was rebuilt in 1865. *The Crucifixion* is by Dante Rossetti, *The Entombment* is by Ford Madox Brown, *The Baptism* and *The Lamb and the Angels* is by Burne-Jones. *The Last Supper, The Maries and the Sepulchre* and *The Ascension* are by William Morris.

B This old quarry provided stone for Carisbrooke Castle.

WOLVERTON MANOR

4 miles (6.4 km) Moderate

You can hardly fail to have a good walk if you visit the church of St. Peter in Shorwell first – there is a medieval wall painting of St. Christopher to bring you luck!

Your path leads past an Elizabethan mansion and across a withy bed (wetland used for growing willow shoots for basketwork) where a Civil War trooper sank to his death (there is a board walk now). By contrast, the views over the coast from the ridgeway are extensive.

6 *Continue along the path which turns right through a gate and left past an old lime pit on your right. Do not take a gate on your left. Climb to a signpost and turn right along the ridgeway (the Worsley Trail). Go ahead through a gate, then bear right through a gate downhill.*

7 *Go through a waymarked gate down to the valley floor and turn left. Turn right in a corner, then go left. **Do not cross a stile in the next corner.** Go right to a gate and descend to the narrow path back to the road (Walkers Lane, the B3399). Turn left along it back to the church.*

1 *Start from the church of St. Peter, Shorwell. Shorwell is at the junction of the B3323 and the B3399, 5 miles (8 km) south of Newport. The no 1B bus (Alum Bay to Ryde) stops nearby at the Crown Inn, Shorwell, and there is a car park opposite the village hall in Russell Road.*
Walk from the church to this junction and bear left up Farriers Way. Turn right up Fine Lane. Maintain your direction up Butts Way and along the signposted path SW4.

Limerstone Down

5 *Go through the waymarked gate and walk with a hedge on your right. Turn right through a gate and turn left immediately to follow a fence on your left. Go ahead along an enclosed path to a gate.*

4 *Veer left to a gate in the top left corner of the field, **but do not go through it!** Turn right to walk with a fence on your left. Continue through a gate in the corner ahead. Walk beside a fence on your left to a waymarked gate. Turn left through it and bear right to a road.*

Go right and turn left up the signposted paths SW6 and 7. Take a narrow path to a gate, go through it and bear left along path SW6. Climb to a waymarked gate tucked in a corner below the top corner gate.

Shorwell

3 *Go ahead through a gate and bear right as waymarked for 20 yards (18 m). Turn left over a footbridge and turn right immediately along a path which bears left through*

marshy woodland (on boardwalks in places). Emerge across a footbridge and over a subsequent stile.

2 *Walk with a fence on your left to a gate in the corner. Continue up a fenced path to reach a road. Turn right along the signposted path SW5 to pass Wolverton Manor.*

A The church of St. Peter in Shorwell houses a magnificent wall painting of St. Christopher over its north door. Believed to date from 1440, it shows the saint renouncing the devil and enlisting in the service of Christ.

B Wolverton Manor is a working farm built during the reign of Queen Elizabeth I (hence its E shape). It is supposedly haunted by the ghost of a murdered fiddler. A bedroom at the back overlooks the old withy bed (now called Trooper's Wood) and is thought to be haunted by the trooper who sank to his death there. The heavy footsteps of the trooper are believed to have been heard for centuries.

Walk 20

BILLINGHAM MANOR

5.5 miles (8.9 km) Easy

Chillerton Down TV mast is a prominent landmark on this walk. It is set in beautiful surroundings with breathtaking views on your right, and with the sea on your left as you take the ridgeway back to Shorwell. Part of the Worsley Trail is walked in the first half of this route, and the path back from Billingham Manor to Bucks Farm is part of the Shepherds Trail.

2 *Avoid a fork on your right. Go ahead through a waymarked gate at the end of the field. Continue beside a fence on your right. Go ahead through a gate in the corner to the next field where you take a gate on the right at the end.*

3 *Bear right to walk with a hedge on your left to a gate. Turn sharply right down towards a farm but veer left to a signpost before it. Turn left up path SW15, climbing with a fence on your right. Go ahead through two gates.*

4 *Keep beside the fence on your right and go through a gate in the far corner of the field, with the TV mast above on your left. Continue to a waymarked gate and turn right along a track. Bear left to a road, turn right along it to a bus stop and fork left up a lane. Turn right at a signpost to follow path G15, walking with a fence, then woodland, then a hedge on your right. Turn right through a waymarked gate and go left beside a fence on your left to a gate leading to an enclosed, grassy, track.*

New Barn Farm

Church

Shorwell

Ⓐ

1 *Shorwell is 5 miles (8 km) south-west of Newport on the B3323. Motorists will easily find a small parking area on the left at the northern entrance to the village. There is a bus stop (1B Alum Bay to Ryde) at the same end of the village, at the foot of the hill called Shorwell Shute. The walk starts here.*
Look for an old water pump close to the bus stop, and a signpost near it. Go up the signposted bridleway SW14 to Northcourt Down, veering right up an enclosed path between gardens to a gate onto the hillside. Bear right, go through a gate and continue above the trees on your right.

Bucks Farm

B3399

Billingham Manor

Ⓑ

6 *Go right, pass the signposted Shepherds Trail on your left, turn right up path SW47 and walk past woods on your left uphill to a ridgeway. Go left to Shorwell, with a fence on your left. Go ahead over two stiles back to the village. Turn right for the start of the walk.*

5 *Ignore a waymarked gate on your left but go through a gate ahead, turn left and follow a fence on your left to a road. Go left and turn right up the signposted path SW43. Continue for just over 0.5 mile (1 km) and bear left to a roadside signpost.*

A Chillerton Down TV mast is 750 feet (230 m) high and was erected in 1958.

B Billingham has the reputation of being the most haunted manor on the Isle of Wight. The most famous spectre is the severed head of King Charles I.

Walk 21
WHALE CHINE
5.5 miles (8.9 km) Easy

Chale Bay was known as the 'Bay of Death', with 60 ships lost here between 1746 and 1808. You can enjoy a grandstand view of its forbidding splendour from the clifftop path between two chines (deep ravines), and remember the heroism of the Lifeboatmen who carried out so many brave rescues.

A Whale Chine is spectacular – a miniature Grand Canyon. It acquired its name when a whale was stranded on its beach.

B This stretch of coastline has seen a string of famous shipwrecks. These include the New York barque *Alpheus Marshall* on 9th February, 1879. She had been sailing from Nova Scotia to London when she was driven onto the Atherfield Ledge. After an epic launch, the Grange Chine lifeboat *Rescue* reached her shattered hull. Coxswain James Buckett was unable to get close, so the 14 crew were rescued by rope. The lifeboat then found itself unable to land in the heavy sea. Instead, the 27 men on board were washed out of the boat and somehow swept ashore. Coxswain Buckett (aged 74), who retired after that, became a folk hero. He had been a smuggler in his youth and was caught, tried and sentenced to five years in the Navy. On his discharge he was rated as Captain of the Fore Top. In his 20 years as Coxswain of the Grange Chine lifeboat he saved a total of 280 lives. There was a further sequel to the wreck of the *Alpheus Marshall* when large tins of beef, prawns and tomatoes were washed ashore from her cargo. This flotsam was soon hidden from the coastguards by the locals. Many a poor family counted it as a Godsend.

The next victim of the Atherfield Ledge, the *Atlas*, came on 25th November, 1880. The brand new Grange Chine lifeboat the *Worcester Cadet*, under the new coxwain Moses Munt, was launched but drifted to leeward. Then the Atherfield coastguards tried and failed to reach the *Atlas*, a 554 ton Austrian barque carrying maize from New York to Germany. In desperation, one of her crew tied a tub to a long rope and tossed it over the side. The tub caught on some rocks, where a brave coastguard secured it and the crew were hauled to safety.

The biggest wreck so far in this area came on 3rd January, 1884, when the 4,426 ton *Duke of Westminster* came ashore on the rocks at Atherfield. The captain had followed faulty bearings in thick fog after steaming from Australia to London with a cargo that included oranges and coconuts (later to add variety to the diets of those on shore), 20 passengers and a large crew of 102. Passengers and crew were taken off by the lifeboat *Worcester Cadet* and, weeks later, the badly damaged ship was towed to London for repairs.

When the 1,588 ton *Sirenia* ran onto Atherfield Ledge on 9th March, 1888, it caused the most dramatic and tragic rescue attempt yet. The captain's wife, woman servant and three children were rescued first. Going back to rescue the captain and his 25 crew, the *Worcester Cadet* was capsized and lost her coxswain, Moses Munt, and Thomas Cotton, the second coxswain. The Brook Lifeboat, the *William Slaney Lewis* then tried, only to lose Reuben Cooper, its second coxswain. The *Worcester Cadet* returned with a scratch crew to complete the rescue. The sum of £1200 was raised to set up a new lifeboat station at Atherfield.

Atherfield's new lifeboat, the *Catherine Swift*, was soon in action. It helped to rescue 227 passengers, 167 crew, 500 sacks of mail and eight and a half tons of silver and gold from the German luxury liner S S *Eider* on 31 January, 1892. The rescue was hailed around the world.

Over

0   1 mile

0   1 km

3 *Cross the A3055 Military Road with care and take the signposted path SW22a (Shepherds Trail) ahead. Veer slightly left across a field to a stile in the fence ahead. Cross it and follow the right hand edge of the next field. Bear left at a corner, then cross a bridge over the ditch on your right. Veer slightly right along the track between fields.*

4 *Turn right along the signposted path SW22 (Shepherds Trail) to Atherfield Road. Turn right to follow this quiet road for nearly 2 miles (3.2 km).*

5 *Pass Atherfield Farm House on your left. Turn right along the signposted path SW55 back to the Military Road. Turn left back to the start of the walk.*

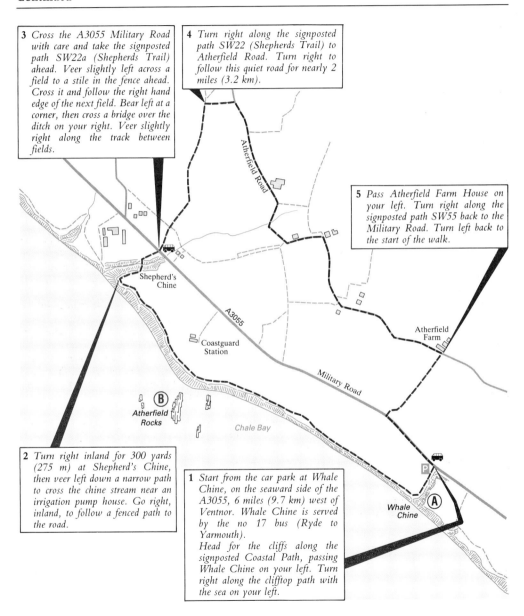

Atherfield Road

Shepherd's Chine

A3055

Coastguard Station

Atherfield Farm

Military Road

Atherfield Rocks

B

Chale Bay

Whale Chine

A

2 *Turn right inland for 300 yards (275 m) at Shepherd's Chine, then veer left down a narrow path to cross the chine stream near an irrigation pump house. Go right, inland, to follow a fenced path to the road.*

1 *Start from the car park at Whale Chine, on the seaward side of the A3055, 6 miles (9.7 km) west of Ventnor. Whale Chine is served by the no 17 bus (Ryde to Yarmouth).*
Head for the cliffs along the signposted Coastal Path, passing Whale Chine on your left. Turn right along the clifftop path with the sea on your left.

ST. CATHERINE'S HILL

4 miles (6.4 km) Moderate

The climb up from Blackgang to Gore Cliff sets the scene for a dramatic walk. Above you, on the left, is the 'pepperpot' (the remains of a lighthouse and oratory) on St. Catherine's Hill. At 775 feet (236 m), this is almost the highest point on the island, with views to match. Below, on the right, is the new lighthouse and the Undercliff. This jumbled landscape had a road through it until a massive fall of rock on 26th July, 1928, wiped it off the map.

A Blackgang was reputedly once the home of a cannibal giant. During the 17th and 18th centuries it was the refuge of a band of notorious smugglers, who gave it its name. It is slowly crumbling into the sea. You can visit the Blackgang Chine Theme Park with its 35 acres (14 hectares) of clifftop gardens. These are floodlit every evening between June and September, and are open Jun – Sept daily 10am - 10pm, Apr – May and Oct daily 10am - 5pm. Admission charge.

B Shipwrecks abound on these rocks, with the most famous being that of the *Clarendon* on 11th October, 1836. This fine, three-masted ship of 345 tons was bound from the West Indies with a cargo of rum, sugar, turtles, coconuts and arrowroot. Also aboard were a crew of 14 and 10 passengers. Hurricane force winds drove the ship onto the rocks, close enough for two crewmen to jump to safety. Tragically, the ship broke up with the fourth wave to hit her: a third crewman was saved but the rest perished. All the bodies were washed ashore, except one. The story is that the sea carried the body of one passenger, Miss Gourley, back to the foot of her father's garden – in Southsea. Work on a lighthouse soon began.

C The new lighthouse was built at the foot of the cliff, just 72 feet (22 m) above sea level. This was to overcome the problem of hill fog. Its height of 107 feet (32 m) allowed it to shine deep into the Channel. The new St. Catherine's lighthouse began operating in March 1840, but there were still shipwrecks. Even smugglers came to grief on the rocks of Rocken End. The brig *Russie* was wrecked on Easter Sunday, 1902. Her cargo of wine, spirits and tobacco was poured away by the coastguards, to the grief of the locals. The old royal yacht *Britannia* also lies somewhere off St Catherine's, being deliberately sunk there after the death of her owner, King George V.

D The 'pepperpot' on top of the hill is the remains of a lighthouse and oratory built in 1328 by the Lord of Chale, William de Godeton, as a penance set by the pope. He had taken advantage of the crew of the shipwrecked *St. Mary of Bayonne* on 22nd April, 1313. She had been bound for the monastery of Livers in Picardy from Bayonne in Gascony with a cargo of 147 barrels of white wine when she had been blown off course and into the clutches of the said lord. William 'bought' 53 surviving barrels at a bargain price. He did his penance, building a curious lighthouse – octagonal outside but quadrangular inside. It was nearly 36 feet (11 m) high, with a pyramidal roof. It is dedicated to St. Catherine. A hermitage had already existed here, but priests were to pray at the oratory and keep the beacon burning for 212 years, until Henry VIII's reign.

E This is the base of a second lighthouse, begun in 1785. It wasn't completed, after being considered too high, and subject to mist and fog.

Over

0   1 mile
0   1 km

4 *Turn left up Pan Lane. Continue along path NT53 to St Catherine's Down.* **Do not** *take a waymarked stile on your right, but bear left along a track. Continue over a cattle grid and through a gate. Follow the blue waymark arrow to go through a gate.*

5 *Turn left to walk beside a fence on your left up to St. Catherine's Oratory.*

6 *Descend from the Oratory, veering slightly right towards the sea. Cross a stile and veer left to a stile which has lost its fence. Go down to cross another stile (in a fence, this time) and follow a fence on your right down to the road. Cross a stile on your right and go down steps to the road.*

7 *Go to the back of a car park and climb steps to a narrow path. Follow this to the Coastal Path and turn right to retrace your steps back to Blackgang Chine.*

St Catherine's Hill
St Catherine's Oratory

Niton Down

Niton

A3055

Rocken End

Lighthouse
St Catherine's Point

1 *Start from the giant figure of a smuggler, with your back to the entrance of Blackgang Chine. This is down the access road to the chine, and car park, on the seaward side of the A3055 near the southern tip of the island. Buses no 16 from Newport and 17 from Ryde both stop here.*
Go right past the Ship Ashore Inn, fork left at a road junction and turn right through a car park. Go up the steps in its top right corner. Cross a stile and take a narrow path up steps ahead. Pass a grassy area on your left and continue up more steps. Reach the clifftop, ignore a path on your left and go ahead along the Coastal Path with the sea on your right.

2 *Look for Rocken End, a large offshore rock that is home to a colony of cormorants, and the lighthouse at St. Catherine's Point on your right.* **Ignore** *a signposted path on your right down to the Old Blackgang Road. Go ahead over a stile and pass the Telecom transmitting station.*

3 *Go ahead over two more stiles, then turn left over another stile to walk inland beside a fence on your right. Cross a stile in the far corner of a field and veer left as waymarked to a stile in a hollow. Cross this to reach a road and go right. Fork left to the church.*

HOY'S MONUMENT

4.5 miles (7.2 km) Moderate

0 ‖———————————————————— 1 mile

0 ‖————————————————— 1 km

It is quite an energetic climb up to Hoy's Monument, but well worth it. The monument itself is a simple column, 72 feet (22 m) high, with a ball on its top. It commands a magnificent view over the island.

6 *Go ahead through the stone gate posts and turn right up a path between bushes. Reach a junction and go left to a road. Take path C28 ahead. Go through a gate and cross the lawns of Pyle Manor. Go into Windmill Copse, bearing left at a fork and emerge at a field.*

7 *Go right over two stiles to a gate leading to a lane, which you go right along for 100 yards (90 m). Bear left along path C24 to a lane. Continue along the signposted path C33 with a hedge on your left (do not take a stile in it). Take a lane on your left back to the Post Office in Chale Green.*

1 *Start from the Post Office at Chale Green. Bus no 16 between Sandown and Newport stops here. Cars can be parked in a lay-by off a minor road near its junction with the B3399 just to the north.*
With your back to the Post Office, go right to the road junction, cross a bridge and turn right along the signposted path to St. Catherine's Down. Walk with a ditch and a hedge on your right. Go ahead over two stiles. Cross a third stile to join a bridleway through a small wood.

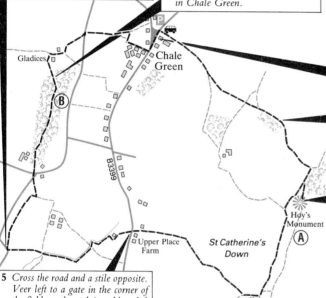

2 *Emerge at a gate and go right along an enclosed path. Go through a gate at the top, turn right and fork left up to Hoy's Monument.*

3 *Retrace your steps to the lower path and turn sharply left along it, with a hedge on your right. Do not turn right through a gate. Go ahead along path C5 with a fence on your right. Ignore an uphill fork on your left. Go ahead along a narrow path between trees. Turn right over a stile and turn left immediately to walk with a fence on your left to a stile ahead. Cross this and turn right to follow a fence on your right.*

5 *Cross the road and a stile opposite. Veer left to a gate in the corner of the field, go through it and bear left beside a ditch on your right. Cross a waymarked stile and walk to cross a stile in the next corner. Step across a stream, cross a stile into the next field and join a driveway.*

4 *Go ahead over two stiles, then cross a third and continue with a hedge on your left. Go ahead across a stile, then over a stile beside a gate and continue to a road.*

A Michael Hoy, of the nearby 'Hermitage', constructed this fine monument 'to commemorate the visit of His Imperial Majesty Alexander I, Emperor of All the Russias, to Great Britain in the year 1814, and in memory of many happy years' residence in his dominions'.

B The high fences passed on your right in Windmill Copse are to keep in deer.

NITON AND WHITWELL

4 miles (6.4 km) Easy

This route covers an attractive stretch of coastline between two interesting old villages. Both places were important in ancient times, long before taxes on brandy, silk, tea or tobacco made smuggling the main occupation in these parts. Niton was a major trading post of the Ancient Britons, when the Isle of Wight was known to them as Ictis. Whitwell was a place of pilgrimage and healing.

> **4** Ignore path NT31 on your left, but go to your right along path NT26, passing houses and a school on your left. Reach a path junction and go ahead along the signposted path NT20. Pass between houses and along Allotment Road. Continue along a track, bearing left at a fork to pass Lower Fields on your right. Follow Ashknowle Lane back to Whitwell. The church is on your left.

> **1** Start from St. Rhadegund's Church, Whitwell. This is near the bus stop for the no 16 between Sandown and Newport. Cars should be parked considerately in the village.
> Go right along Ventnor Road, passing the youth hostel on your right. Bear right up the lane signposted 'St. Rhadegund's Footpath'. When this bears right to a Telecom Transmitting Station, go ahead over a stile.

> **3** Ignore a path bearing right over a stile. Follow the Coastal Path as it bends right. Ignore the signposted path NT30 on your left.

> **2** Turn right along the Coastal Path, walking with the sea on your left. Maintain your direction over a stile.

A Niton's parish church is dedicated to St. Rhadegund (pronounced Redgun). She was a German princess, the daughter of Bortaire, King of Thuringia, and had lived in France for several years when she was taken captive at the age of 10. Married unwillingly at the age of 18 to Clotaire, King of Soissons, she withdrew from court and devoted herself to the relief of the poor. She took the veil in 594 at Poitiers.

B The curved bay below Niton is called Puckaster Cove, which was most probably a port in Roman times. The chief trade of the Ancient Britons was in tin, mined in Cornwall. Diodorus Siculus recorded in 25 BC that the tin was carried at low tide in carts to an island called Ictis, which is probably a corruption of Vectis, the Roman name for the Isle of Wight. Many believe that the Solent was fordable then. Both the Phoenicians and the Greeks came to Britain for tin. There is substantial place name evidence of an Ancient British road from Cornwall to Lepe in Hampshire, beside which Greek and Roman coins have been found. There was a Roman building at Gurnard, the nearest point on the Isle of Wight to Lepe, and a farm near Puckaster was called Buddle, which is also the name of a frame used to wash tin ore.

King Charles II was driven ashore at Puckaster Cove whilst yachting in 1675.

ROBIN HILL

2 miles (3.2 km) Easy

```
0                                           1 mile
|----------|----------|----------|----------|
0                              1 km
```

This short walk could be combined with a visit to the Robin Hill Country Park. You gain a free view of part of this from over the fence beside your right of way. The second field on your right in the Country Park has ostriches, rheas and llamas, plus lots of rabbits. You can also hear the ducks and geese as you pass Combley Farm.

2 Turn right up the signposted path N19. Go through a gate and walk with a hedge on your left and a fence on your right. Continue through a gate and descend gradually to a field corner. Go ahead between two hedges to emerge at a gate.

3 Go through the gate and walk beside the hedge on your right. Continue through a gate in the corner and turn right along a track.

4 Go through the farmyard at Combley Farm and follow the track as it bends right. Continue through a gate, over a cattle grid and bear left.

Combley Farm

Ⓐ ⬜ Roman Villa Ⓑ

Ⓟ
🚌 ⬜
Robin Hill Country Park

Gallows Hill

Ⓒ

5 Go right over a cattle grid in the top right corner and follow the hedged track to a road. Bear right along it back to the Hare & Hounds.

1 Start from the Hare & Hounds Inn, which is at a road junction 3 miles (4.8 km) east of Newport. Buses stop here (nos 3 & 3A between Sandown and Newport, no 8 between Sandown and Ryde). There is roadside parking close to the inn.

Go right to pass the entrance to Robin Hill Country Park on your right. Bear right along Briddlesford Road at a fork. Pass the signposted path N92 on your left. Go ahead 100 yards (90 m).

A Robin Hill Country Park has a toboggan ride, safari cars, a Santa Fé railway, BMX bikes, archery, shooting, assault courses, a nine-hole golf course (tee off from an island in the lake), an amusement arcade plus lots of trees and animals. It covers 80 acres (32 hectares) of downland and is open Mar - Oct daily 10am - 5pm. Admission charge.

B This corner of the Park is occupied by a recently excavated Roman villa.

C A St. Helens doctor was driving past Gallows Hill on 4th January, 1969, when he reported the night lit up with a tremendously bright light. He and his wife claimed they saw about 100 figures bearing torches running across the road. One wore a long jerkin with a wide leather belt. He passed right through the bonnet of their car and vanished. Were these the ghostly torchbearers of a Roman legion? Or were they connected with the Bronze Age round barrows on the hill? Secondary Saxon burials were found high in one of them in 1815.

Another story connected with this place concerns Micah Moorey. He was hanged at Winchester in 1776 and his body was hung up here, as a deterrent to would be felons.

Walk 26
FIRESTONE COPSE
2 miles (3.2 km) Easy

This well-waymarked route is a joy in all seasons, following pleasant woodland paths shaded by oak trees, and with Wootton Mill Pond adding variety. Wildlife abounds – but please don't pick the wild daffodils or primroses if you come here during spring. The green waymarks make navigation easy.

5 When you reach a green waymark post near a plantation of conifers, turn right to reach a wide forest track. Turn left as indicated by a green waymark post. Turn right as waymarked at a crosstracks.

6 Follow the green waymarks, taking a track on your left to a T junction. Go left back to the car park.

2 At a track junction, take a wide, gravel track on your left.

1 Start from the car park in Firestone Copse. This is reached from Firestone Copse Road, a quiet lane linking Fishbourne with Havenstreet, where the nearest bus stops are. For this reason, if you rely on public transport it would make sense to combine this route with Walk **27** (Quarr Abbey), which starts from the bus stop in Havenstreet (bus nos 7 & 7A from Yarmouth to Ryde, 8 from Ryde to Sandown).
Look for the official entrance to Firestone Copse, on your left as you go north from Havenstreet, and go left to the official car park. Look for the Information Board and go right 10 yards (9 m) then left at a 'Forest Walk' sign to follow the route with the green waymarks.

4 When the gravel track bends sharply right, bear left along a path into the conifers. There is a green waymark post near a seat at its start. Continue through oak trees and beside the creek on your left.

3 Ignore a path waymarked with red on your left. Continue ahead.

Havenstreet

A Firestone Copse belongs to the Forestry Commission and covers 247 acres (100 hectares). The early plantings were of conifers, such as Corsican pine, Douglas fir and Lawson Cypress, but oak trees (the natural climax vegetation) have also been planted since the 1930s. There should be some fine stands of oak in the 21st century, while the conifers are thinned every five years for local timber needs, such as fencing and fuel.

B Wootton Mill Pond is home to herons throughout the year, and waders come here in the winter.

Walk 27
QUARR ABBEY
6.5 miles (10.5 km) Easy

This route is mostly along good, firm, tracks. Trees often provide shade or shelter, and you may spot a train of the Isle of Wight Steam Railway. The essentially peaceful, relaxing, nature of the surroundings is epitomised by links with both the ruined Quarr Abbey and its modern replacement. This walk could well be combined with the short Walk **26** in Firestone Copse, joining it just after point 2.

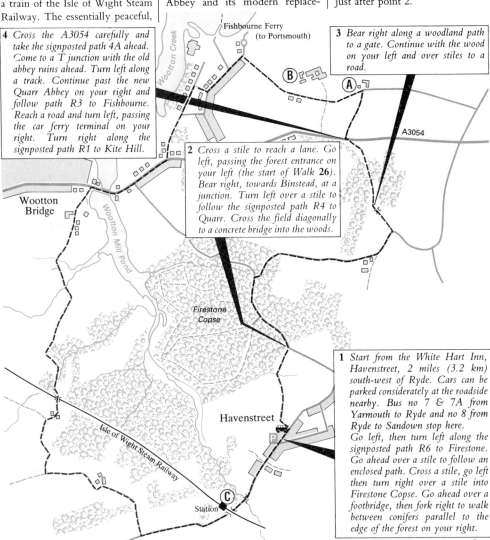

4 *Cross the A3054 carefully and take the signposted path 4A ahead. Come to a T junction with the old abbey ruins ahead. Turn left along a track. Continue past the new Quarr Abbey on your right and follow path R3 to Fishbourne. Reach a road and turn left, passing the car ferry terminal on your right. Turn right along the signposted path R1 to Kite Hill.*

3 *Bear right along a woodland path to a gate. Continue with the wood on your left and over stiles to a road.*

2 *Cross a stile to reach a lane. Go left, passing the forest entrance on your left (the start of Walk 26). Bear right, towards Binstead, at a junction. Turn left over a stile to follow the signposted path R4 to Quarr. Cross the field diagonally to a concrete bridge into the woods.*

1 *Start from the White Hart Inn, Havenstreet, 2 miles (3.2 km) south-west of Ryde. Cars can be parked considerately at the roadside nearby. Bus no 7 & 7A from Yarmouth to Ryde and no 8 from Ryde to Sandown stop here.*
Go left, then turn left along the signposted path R6 to Firestone. Go ahead over a stile to follow an enclosed path. Cross a stile, go left then turn right over a stile into Firestone Copse. Go ahead over a footbridge, then fork right to walk between conifers parallel to the edge of the forest on your right.

Fishbourne Ferry
(to Portsmouth)

Wootton Creek

A3054

Wootton Bridge

Wootton Mill Pond

Firestone Copse

Havenstreet

Isle of Wight Steam Railway

Station

Over

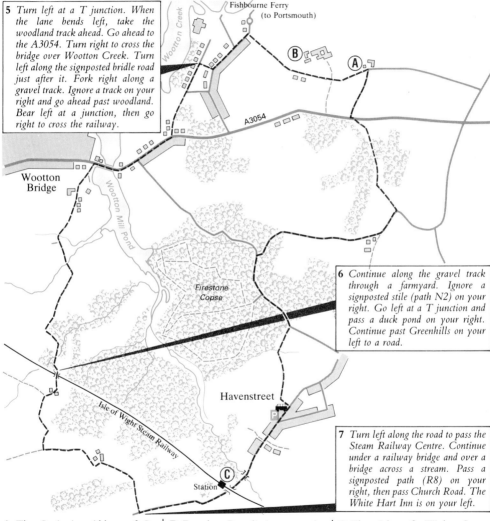

5 *Turn left at a T junction. When the lane bends left, take the woodland track ahead. Go ahead to the A3054. Turn right to cross the bridge over Wootton Creek. Turn left along the signposted bridle road just after it. Fork right along a gravel track. Ignore a track on your right and go ahead past woodland. Bear left at a junction, then go right to cross the railway.*

6 *Continue along the gravel track through a farmyard. Ignore a signposted stile (path N2) on your right. Go left at a T junction and pass a duck pond on your right. Continue past Greenhills on your left to a road.*

7 *Turn left along the road to pass the Steam Railway Centre. Continue under a railway bridge and over a bridge across a stream. Pass a signposted path (R8) on your right, then pass Church Road. The White Hart Inn is on your left.*

A The Savigniac Abbey of St. Mary was founded in 1132 by Baldwin de Redvers. It became Cistercian in 1147 and was dissolved in 1536.

B French Benedictine monks began building Quarr Abbey in 1907, and it gained its official status 30 years later.

C The Isle of Wight Steam Railway runs from Havenstreet to Wootton, and is to be extended to Smallbrook.

ARRETON MANOR
5.5 miles (8.9 km) Easy

Two manor houses ensure that this walk will take a whole day to complete, should you visit them both. They are well worth their admission fees, and refreshments are also available. St. George's Church adds extra interest, with the climb up Arreton Down bringing the reward of excellent views.

A St. George's Church, Arreton, has a Saxon foundation, but was rebuilt by the monks of Quarr Abbey in the 14th century, with a farmhouse and a tithe barn. Look in the churchyard for the graves of Elizabeth Warbridge, the heroine of *The Dairyman's Daughter* by Legh Richmond, and her sister Hannah.

B Arreton Manor claims to be the most beautiful and intriguing house on the island. It is certainly built on an historic site. Spearheads and socketed daggers dating back 3500 years have been found above it on Arreton Down, where there are ancient burial mounds. Roman coins, pottery and armour have also been unearthed. The present house is mostly Elizabethan, but incorporates some parts of the farmhouse built by the monks of Quarr Abbey in the 14th century. The manor once belonged to King Alfred the Great. It came into the possession of Quarr Abbey in about 1156 and was leased by the last abbot to John Leigh in 1525. King Charles I came here several times, reviewing troops in 1628 and knighting John Leigh on another occasion. The king's snuff box is still here. You can also see a delightful collection of dolls, toys and dolls houses, including the Pomeroy Regency Dolls House. There is also a wireless museum and a lace museum. Refreshments can be obtained in a delightful Jacobean tea room, with gardens and a pottery and gift shop nearby. Arreton Manor is open from the week before Easter to the end of October, Mon - Fri 10am - 6pm, Sun 2 - 6pm (closed Sat). Admission charge.

C This is part of the Bembridge Trail, a 15 mile (24 km) route between Newport and Bembridge Point.

D This dismantled railway used to be the line which linked Sandown with Newport in a wide loop. Originally known as the Isle of Wight (Newport Junction) Railway, it became part of the Isle of Wight Central Railway. Trains ran along it from 1879 to 1956.

E Haseley Manor was recorded in the Domesday Book of 1086. William the Conqueror passed it to his son, William Rufus, who died in mysterious circumstances in the New Forest. The Norman Baron Engelger de Bohun then acquired Haseley, which was sold to Quarr Abbey in 1136 (the deed of sale is held by the British Museum). The monks used Haseley as a grange and built a fulling mill on the nearby stream. Sheep were kept for their wool, which was stored at Haseley. At the Dissolution, John Myll, the member of parliament for Southampton, rebuilt this house with stone from Quarr Abbey. Haseley eventually fell into the lap of Dowsabelle, the widow of John Myll's son who was famous for her hospitality. The old sea-dog Sir Edward Horsey chose to reside with her instead of at Carisbrooke Castle when Elizabeth I made him the captain or governor of the island. Mistress Dowsabelle also consoled him for a wife absent in France. Sir Edward died of the plague in 1582, and Dowsabelle started a finishing school for young ladies. On her death in 1603 the estate became the property of Thomas Fleming, who was knighted and made Chief Baron of the Exchequer in 1604. He was one of Guy Fawkes' judges and became Chief Prosecutor in 1607. The estate managed to stay intact within the Fleming family until 1952. Visitors can see both pottery, and sweets, being made here. Open Apr - Sept daily 10am - 6pm, Oct - Mar Mon - Fri 10am - 6pm. Admission charge.

Over

Walk 28
ARRETON MANOR
Continued

1 *Start from the White Lion pub in Arreton, which is on the A3056, 4 miles (6.4 km) south-east of Newport. Cars can be parked nearby, and bus no 3 (Ryde to Sandown service) stops here. Facing the White Lion, go up a path on your right, between the pub and the church. Walk past the churchyard on your right and up path A12 past Arreton Manor on your left. Climb with a fence on your right to a stile. Cross it and bear left, ignoring the first path on your right, then bear right up the second path. Pass a chalk pit on your left and reach a road at a gate.*

2 *Turn right just before the gate to walk on the down with a fence on your left until you reach a gate in it. Bear right at the gate downhill to a hedge. Go left, reach an old chalk pit on your left and turn right through a waymarked gate. Go down a track past the signposted path A9 on your right. Take the next turning on your left, forking left with it to a lane.*

3 *Go right along the lane. Ignore a turning to Ryde soon afterwards on your left. Pass Langbridge Chapel on your right, then turn right along the signposted path NC8 towards Horringford.*

4 *Take the turning on your right towards Haseley Manor. Go left over a signposted stile to a footbridge on your right. Turn right over this and go right around the edge of a field to join the access lane to the manor.*

5 *Go left along the lane to a road. Turn right for a few paces and then turn left to cross the road carefully to a signposted path alongside Arbutus Cottage. Go ahead over a small field and a stile in the corner ahead. Walk with a fence on your right to a stile in it. **Don't cross it**, but veer left down the field to cross two footbridges. Then climb to take a gate ahead. Walk with a fence on your left to a gate.*

6 *Go ahead through the gate to pass a wood on your right. Now fix your gaze on the top of the other side of the valley on your right. Look for a stile, with another below it. Continue ahead until there is a gap into the field on your right. Turn right through it and along a path over the two stiles spotted earlier. Go ahead to join a road near the school, then go left back to the White Lion.*

45

APPULDURCOMBE HOUSE

5 miles (8 km) Moderate/strenuous; muddy after rain

A picturesque, if commercialised, village is the start for a varied walk along tracks, up a steep hill and through woodland. The view from the Worsley memorial is one of the best on the island, with a magnificent sweep taking in Sandown Bay in the east and the cliffs of Tennyson Down in the west. You should allow plenty of time to visit all the various attractions.

A Godshill now caters for the coach parties who come here. There is an Old Smithy, a Natural History Centre, a Toy Museum and a highly recommended Model Village which is open Apr – Sept daily 10am – 5pm, Oct daily 10.30am – 4pm. Admission charge. The real glory of Godshill is its church. Legend states how it was planned for a lower site, but the stones kept being inexpicably moved overnight to the top of the hill, a site considered sacred for many thousands of years. Outside are a 15th-century churchyard cross and an 18th-century sundial. Inside there is a unique medieval wall painting of Jesus on a triple-branched flowering lily – the Lily Cross.

B Appuldurcombe House was the home of the Worsley family. A wife in this family once complained that she had only 27 lovers when her husband accused her of taking 34. The grounds were landscaped by 'Capability' Brown. The house, now just an empty shell, is in the care of English Heritage, and is open Easter – Sept daily 10am – 6pm, Oct – Easter Tues – Sun 10am – 4pm. Admission charge.

C This obelisk is a memorial to Sir Robert Worsley, who rebuilt the Tudor house between 1702 and 1712. It was erected by Sir Richard Worsley in 1774. Severely damaged by lightning in 1831, it was restored (but not to its original height of 70 feet or 21 m) in 1983.

Godshill

Over

0   1 mile

0   1 km

2 Retrace your steps to the Griffin Inn and go ahead past it towards Shanklin. Turn right through a gate beside a cattle grid to follow the signposted path GL44 to Freemantle Gate. This begins as a metalled lane, but when that bends left to Godshill Park Farm, go ahead through a waymarked gate along a track. Pass a signposted path (GL56) to Sainham on your right. Pass the signposted path GL43 to Redhill Lane on your left, after an old mill pond.

1 Start from the Griffin Inn, Godshill, on the A3020 between Newport and Shanklin. There is a car park opposite. Bus nos 2 (Cowes to Sandown), 2A (Newport to Ventnor) and 8 Sandown to Ryde) stop here.
Face the Griffin Inn and go right into the village. Turn left at a road junction and fork right up a path to the church of All Saints.

3 Go ahead past woodland on your right to reach Freemantle Gate. You will return here, but meanwhile go ahead through the gate and beside a fence on your right to a signpost. Veer right along path GL47 towards Appuldurcombe House. Cross a stile beside a gate in the corner of the field and walk with a fence now on your left to a stile beside a gate in the next field corner. Pass Appuldurcombe Farm on your right and go ahead along a track to a gate. The entrance to Appuldurcombe House is opposite if you wish to visit.

5 Go through the gate and turn left along the signposted path GL49, a woodland track. Turn left over a stile in the wall to follow the signposted path GL63. This climbs a steep hill then bears right. Walk with a fence on your left to the obelisk, on your right. Bear left towards the radio mast, crossing a stile and reaching another stile with a signpost beside it.

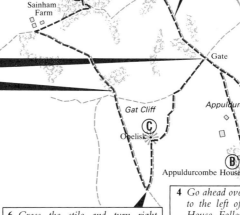

7 Continue through a high deer gate and past a deer fence on your right to another deer gate. Go through to follow the fenced track to Sainham Deer Farm. Turn right through a deer gate to pass the farm on your left. Walk along the signposted path GL56 into Beech Copse ahead. Ignore the path forking left down through the trees. Take the broader path to a junction and then turn sharply left into the trees. The path descends and bears right to a stile. Go ahead with trees on your left back to Godshill, turning right when you come to a lane, to return to the Griffin Inn.

6 Cross the stile and turn right towards Sainham. Walk with the fence on your right down the steep Gat Cliff. Go through a gate into woodland and take the signposted track GL58.

4 Go ahead over a stile beside a gate to the left of the entrance to the House. Follow the signposted path GL47 which gives a good view of Appuldurcombe House on your right. Turn left along the signposted path GL45 to Redhill Lane, bearing left to the far bottom corner of the field. Go ahead over a stile, the access lane to the House and another stile. Bear left along the signposted path GL44 back to Freemantle Gate.

STENBURY DOWN

5 miles (8 km) Moderate

0   1 mile

0   1 km

Stenbury Down is a great favourite with local ramblers. It is crossed by the 12 mile (20 km) long Stenbury Trail between Newport and Ventnor. Its high chalk ridge gives splendid views, and the lower field paths pass some attractive ponds. Pilgrims and the sick would have walked these ways in medieval times to visit the holy (whit) well at Whitwell, which is passed near the start of this walk.

2 *Turn right up the lane, then go left along the path signposted NT6 to Stenbury Farm. Continue through a gate and along the signposted path GL61, ignoring a path to Newbarn on your right. Turn left over a stile, then turn right immediately to walk with a hedge on your right to a stile in the corner. Go ahead to a stile at the top of the field and follow the hedge round on your right to a footbridge. Cross this and turn left up a track until it nearly reaches a road.*

1 *Start from St. Rhadegund's Church, Whitwell. This is near the bus stop for the no 16 bus between Sandown and Newport. Cars can be parked considerably in the village.*
Go right along Ventnor Road, as far as the youth hostel on your right. Turn left down a bridle road (look for a low signpost for path NT15) between 'Fairways' (a bungalow) and 'Bywell' (a house). Notice the old holy (whit) well on your right, near the old water standard. Go down a field to cross a stream by a footbridge. Veer left to a gate in the next corner (ignoring a stile to the left of it) and follow a narrow path to the right and over the line of an old railway to a gate. Go through the gate to a signpost and turn left along the track NT10 to Nettlecombe Lane.

3 *Turn right up the signposted path GL52. Continue through a gate, ignore a stile on your left and go right along a hedged track. Pass a house on your right, then bear left uphill, ignoring a left turning.*

4 *Reach a path junction and go right uphill. Keep close to a hedge, then a wall on your left. Continue through a waymarked gate in a field corner and aim for the further of two radio masts, passing the nearer one on your left.*

Stenbury Down

Stenbury Manor

Nettlecombe

Whitwell

P

Church

5 *Join the access lane to the radio mast ahead and follow it until it bends left, downhill. Go ahead, ignoring a stile on your right, to reach a signposted stile. Turn right along path NT1. Descend with a fence on your right to a path junction. Go ahead along path NT119 through a gate and with a hedge on your left. Turn right along the signposted path NT5 then left through a waymarked gate.*

6 *Pass ponds on your right and continue to a signpost. Go ahead along path NT13 to retrace your steps to Whitwell.*

A The parish church used to consist of two separate chapels, one dedicated to St. Mary and one to St. Rhadegunde, the patron saint of the De Estur family, the lords of Gatcombe (see Walk **18**).

B The holy well is a little way further from the road than one of the handsome iron water standards erected here by William Spindler in 1887.

C This is the old railway from Ventnor towards Newport.

ST. LAWRENCE

4.5 miles (7.2 km) Moderate

0   1 mile
0   1 km

The St. Lawrence Undercliff was formed by the underlying gault clay sliding down towards the sea, bringing the porous greensand rock with it. The Botanic Gardens have found a good home here, and the smuggling museum is housed in vaults under the A3055. Your path climbs inland for a view over the sea, then zigzags back down.

4 *Bear left along a lane, take the third turning on your right uphill to the Whitwell Road. Continue up the signposted path V60 to Stenbury Down. Fork right along path V62.*

5 *Pass Week Farm and bear left up a track. Turn right along a signposted path to Upper Ventnor. Cross a stile and go right along path V38.*

6 *Pass a golf course on your left and descend towards the sea. Ignore paths going to Ventnor on your left. Reach a road and turn right along it for 300 yards (275 m), then bear left down path V73. Ignore a path to the cliffs on your right.*

7 *Bear left to a road and go left along it (Inglewood Park) to the A3055. Cross this road carefully and turn left to follow the pavement back to the start of the walk.*

1 *Start from the entrance to the car park of the Ventnor Botanical Gardens. This is on the seaward side of the A3055, 1 mile (1.6 km) west of Ventnor. Buses no 16B between Newport and Ryde and 17 between Ryde and Yarmouth both stop here.*
Walk through the car park, passing the Museum of Smuggling History on your right. Continue past the Temperate House on your left and go left to a signpost which points right to the Coastal Footpath and Meadow. Bear right, diagonally, to another signpost and turn right along path V93 to Woody Bay and St Lawrence.

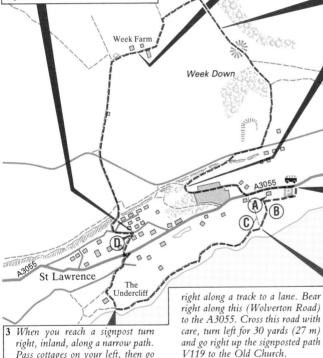

3 *When you reach a signpost turn right, inland, along a narrow path. Pass cottages on your left, then go right along a track to a lane. Bear right along this (Wolverton Road) to the A3055. Cross this road with care, turn left for 30 yards (27 m) and go right up the signposted path V119 to the Old Church.*

2 *Pass Orchard Bay House on your left and the stock yards of the Rare Breeds and Waterfowl Park on your right. Emerge at a clifftop and walk **carefully** along the Coastal Path with the sea on your left.*

A The Museum of Smuggling History is an extensive underground display. Open Easter-Sept daily 9 am - 5 pm. Admission charge.

B Ventnor Botanic Gardens are open daily (free). The Temperate House, with its collection of exotic plants is open Easter - Oct daily 10am - 5pm, Nov - Easter Tues - Thurs 11am - 3pm & Sun 1pm - 4pm. Admission charge.

C The Isle of Wight Rare Breeds & Waterfowl Park is open Easter - Oct daily 10am - 5.30pm. Admission charge.

D The Old Church, St. Lawrence, is a Norman building.

Walk 32
ALVERSTONE
4 miles (6.4 km) Easy

If you enjoy tranquillity, you will find these old tracks splendidly quiet. This valley, the local name of which is the 'vineyard', perhaps referring to the medieval period, has been cultivated for many centuries. Maize and garlic now soak up the sun here, and wild flowers and birds abound near the River Yar. This route can be linked with Walk **34** just after point **10**.

1 *Start from the car park below Ashey Down, about 2 miles (3.2 km) west of Brading. The nearest bus stop is at Brading, so you may wish to combine this walk with Walk **34** (Brading), if you are using public transport. Cross the road from the car park and turn left along a roadside path.*

2 *Turn right down the signposted path NC5, going through a gate into Knighton East Wood. Ignore the signposted path (no 4) on your right.*

3 *Ignore a track into the wood on your right. Go down a hedged track to a crosstracks.*

4 *Turn right along path NC45 towards Knighton (the Bembridge Trail). Bear right through trees and pass the entrance to a sandpit on your right. Take the sandy path ahead, which runs alongside a fence on your right, into woodland. Bear left to a signpost at a junction.*

10 *Follow the fenced track as it swings left to a gate. Go through and turn immediately left along the Downland Way Path, parallel to the road on your right. Retrace your steps to the car park.*

9 *Follow a hedged path to a gate. Go ahead with a hedge on your right only, then veer left up a farm track beside a fence on your left. Go ahead through a gate in the corner of this field to take a fenced track.*

8 *Go through the gate to reach a lane at a corner. Go ahead and to the left up it. When the lane bends left, take the signposted path to Ashey Down ahead.*

7 *Go ahead over a black bridge. Continue for another 220 yards (200 m), then bear left over a stile to take the signposted path B54. Walk with the River Yar on your left. Cross a footbridge near an old mill and follow a hedged path to a road. Go left to a signposted path near the village hall. Turn left along this and bear right after the last house. Go through a gate and continue with a fence on your left to another gate.*

6 *Turn left along the signposted bridleway to Alverstone. Follow the track between fields to an old railway line and go left along it.*

5 *From the junction, bear left to reach a lane. Ignore a turning to Lower Knighton Farm on your left. Continue over a bridge and around right and left bends.*

To Newport

To Brading

Kern Farm

(A) Lower Knighton Farm

(B) River Yar

(C) Alverstone

A Notice the toadstool like 'staddle stones' supporting the 18th-century granary at Lower Knighton Farm. They prevent vermin and damp from spoiling the grain.

B This is a section of the railway that linked Newport and Sandown from 1879 to 1956.

C Alverstone Mill was recorded in the Domesday Book of 1086.

WROXALL

4.5 miles (7.2 km) Moderate

0   1 mile

0   1 km

Come on a clear day to enjoy the stunning views which accompany you for much of this walk. The sense of being on the top of the island is reinforced by the heather and gorse which give the area such an upland appearance. The old ridgeway path provides easy access to inspiring countryside, but the woodland paths have their own charm as you approach St. Martin's Down.

2 Fork right over a stile along the signposted path V30 towards Shanklin. Go ahead with a hedge on your left, cross a stile and take a fenced path to another stile. Go ahead along path V33, ignore a stile on your left but cross a stile beside a gate in the far corner.

3 Follow the path through woodland to a waymarked stile in the fence on your right. Cross it and bear left beside a hedge on your left to a signpost in the next field corner.

4 Turn left into the next field and continue beside a hedge on your left to a stile in the next corner. Do not cross it. Instead, turn right along the signposted path SS12 towards Ventnor. Keep the hedge on your left and cross stiles as you climb uphill to a signpost. Continue along path V40. Bear left through a waymarked gate.

St Martin's Down

Shanklin Down

235m

Wroxall

Church

Ⓐ

Manor Road

Wroxall Manor Farm

Ⓒ

Luccombe Down

Ⓑ

Wroxall Down

235m

☐ Radar station

1 Start from the parish church at Wroxall, near which bus nos 2A (Ventnor to Newport), 16B (Ryde to Newport) stop. Cars may be parked considerately nearby.
With your back to the church, go to the right and turn right up Castle Road. Pass a cemetery on your right, then pass Castle Lane on your left.

7 Bear left along the lane into Wroxall. Pass the Star Inn on your right. Go straight ahead along High Street back to the church on your right.

6 Turn right over the signposted path V8 which leads back to Wroxall. Go down a fenced path, then through Wroxall Copse. Continue down to a lane.

5 Divert over a stile on your left to the summit of Shanklin Down. Return over the stile to maintain your direction along the ridgeway path. Ignore side paths and follow the ridgeway past a radar station.

A The parish church of St. John the Evangelist, Wroxall, was built with stone excavated from the nearby railway tunnel, in 1877.

B This is a Site of Special Scientific Interest. An acid, flinty soil caps the chalk here, resulting in the large area of heather and gorse.

C Wroxall Manor Farm has existed since at least 1086, when the Domesday Book was compiled. Its present buildings date from the 18th century.

BRADING
6 miles (9.7 km) Moderate

Brading has an interesting history and was once a sea port visited by the Romans. This route makes a detour from an attractive woodland path at Kelly's Copse to the remains of a Roman villa. The path to it is over Brading Down, one of the most popular scenic spots on the island. The return path is across the Nunwell estate. Nunwell House is well worth a visit, so allow plenty of time for this walk. This route can be linked with Walk **32** at point **5**.

A The beautiful church of St. Mary is built on the spot where St. Wilfrid converted the pagan inhabitants of the island to Christianity in 685.

B The Isle of Wight Wax Museum is a superb place for tracing the history of the island and enjoying a Chamber of Horrors. Open May - Sept daily 10am - 10pm, Oct - Apr daily 10am - 5pm. Admission charge.

C The Lilliput Antique Doll & Toy Museum is world famous. Open May -Sept daily 9.30am - 9.30pm, Mar - Apr and Oct - Jan daily 10am - 5pm. Admission charge.

D Look for the bullring in the middle of the traffic island. This is where bulls were tethered for baiting. A popular entertainment, this cruelty wasn't outlawed until 1835. Before then, on high days and holidays, the mayor and other civic dignitaries used to assemble here to set a bulldog upon the unfortunate bull.

E Notice Little Jane's Cottage (dated 1547) on your right. Jane Squibb was immortalised by Legh Richmond in his tale 'The Young Cottager' in the famous book *Annals of the Poor*. Stricken with consumption, she died on 30th January, 1799, in her fifteenth year.

F The Devil's Punchbowl is the large round barrow inside the field 150 yards (135 m) to your left as you face the gate leading to the road. Dating from the Bronze Age, it contained a crouched burial (where the corpse is buried in a crouched position, rather than laid out) rather high up in the mound, which suggests to the experts that the primary burial awaits discovery. An antler hammerhead found here is now in the British Museum. Across the road, there are interpretation panels at the viewpoint. These depict the scene below in Roman times, when there was an inlet of the sea reaching almost to the Roman villa. The view was changed by the construction of an embankment in the 19th century.

G Adgestone Vineyard is open Mon - Fri 9am - 4.30pm & Sat 10am - 12.30pm.

H This is one of the finest accessible Roman villas in England, with mosaics that are arguably the best in Britain. Visitors were greeted in the entrance hall by a mosaic of Orpheus, a symbol of welcome and protection. Another room has a mosaic depicting a creature that is half human/half chicken. The *triclinium* or dining-room has mosaics of Perseus and Andromeda, a swastika and the seasons. Medusa has snakes emanating from her hair, while other scenes show Ceres and Triptolemus celebrating the origin of farming, an astrologer pointing with a rod to a globe and King Lycurgus attacking Ambrosia. The villa also had a hypocaust (underfloor heating system) and was inhabited from the third to the fifth centuries. It is open Apr - Sept Mon - Sat 10am - 5.30pm, Sun 10.30am - 5.30pm. Admission charge.

I Nunwell House was the home of the Oglander family from Norman times until 1980. The present house was built in the 16th century and much of the estate was then planted with oak trees. These were felled to build ships during the Napoleonic wars and were not replanted. The island's saddest ghost is reputed to wander the old house. It is the figure of 'Little Missy', Charlotte, the mentally-retarded daughter of the sixth baronet. Nunwell is open Jul - Sept Sun - Thur 10am - 5pm. Admission charge.

Over

0   1 mile

0   1 km

5 *Turn right to walk along the signposted path 26, going into woodland and ignoring a path forking left to a stile. Go ahead through a nature reserve. Take the signposted path B24 to Nunwell at a junction. Cross a stile and go through more woodland. Continue with a hedge on your left, go through a gap and turn right along a woodland path between two fields.*

6 *Go ahead over a stile and maintain your direction to a stile ahead. Continue over a lane to follow the signposted path B23 to Brading. Go ahead across a big field to a road, over stiles and as signposted. Go right past the entrance to Nunwell House, fork right along Doctor's Lane, then left up Cross Street to Brading High Street. Go left back to the start.*

1 *Start from the car park on your left as you enter Brading along the A3055 from Ryde. This is next to St. Mary's Church, where there are bus stops for bus nos 16, 16B & 17 between Ryde and Shanklin). You can also reach Brading by British Rail, direct from Ryde Pier Head.*
Go left to pass the church on your left. Continue down the High Street to the Bullring. Continue up Mall Road.

Nunwell House

A3055

Brading

Station

Brading Down

4 *Go through the gate into the wood and follow the path downhill to its junction with the broad path running along the bottom of the wood. Bear left in the same direction as before. Pass Nunwell House on your right. Go ahead at a path junction along the signposted path B32 towards Newchurch. Pass an old chalk pit on your left. Go through a gate out of the woodland. Walk with a fence on your right, ignore the signposted Nunwell Trail forking left uphill. Follow the hedge on your right until your path bends left around the hillside, climbing gradually. Converge with the Bembridge Trail and take its track past trees on your right. Go through a gate and bear right to a gate beside a signpost in the top right corner of the field. Go through it to the road and turn right.*

Roman Villa

3 *Go ahead across the field to a gate, which leads to a road. Before going through, notice the Bronze Age burial mound on your left. Cross the road and veer left to a car park, with a fine view over Sandown Bay. Go through a gate to descend along the signposted path B42 to Adgestone. Veer left to go through a signposted gate and go down a hedged path. Pass a vineyard on your right, emerge at a lane and go right, then turn sharply left along a lane. Keep left at a junction. Climb steps on your right to a path leading to the Roman villa.*

2 *Turn right up the signposted path 39 (passing Little Jane's Cottage on your right). Continue past an old chalk pit on your left and above trees on your right. Ignore false trails on your right, but fork right along an obvious clear woodland path which gradually descends to the foot of the wood, where you walk with the fence on your right. Ignore a stile (path B27) in the fence and go ahead to pass an avenue of lime trees on your right. Continue for 100 yards (90 m) then turn left up a steep path which bears sharply left through the trees. Emerge at a gate onto a field.*

Retrace your steps to the start of point 3.

Walk 35
SHANKLIN & SANDOWN
3.8 miles (6 km) Moderate

This walk starts from the railway station at Shanklin. The Island Line (or Ryde Rail) is the sole survivor of an extensive network of routes throughout the island. With its fast connections to Portsmouth via the ferry, this line is popular with tourists staying at either Sandown or Shanklin. The cliff walk between the two resorts is justifiably very popular, with views over Sandown Bay. This route can be linked with Walk **36** at point **1**.

5 *Go left to reach the pier, opposite which is Sandown's Tourist Information Centre. Turn left, inland, up Pier Street and bear left up High Street (soon changing its name to Beachfield Road). Turn right at Broadway and visit the parish church. Continue up Broadway to Station Avenue, where you turn left for the British Rail station.*

4 *Pass through Lake Cliff Top Gardens and go along Cliff Walk, then Cliff Road. Reach Ferncliff Gardens and go down a flight of steps, then bear right down a ramp to Sandown Esplanade.*

1 *Start from Shanklin's British Rail station, on the line from Ryde. There is a car park here. If you arrive at the bus station, walk along Languard Road, turn right into Marine Crossroad and then left into Regent Street to reach the start of the walk.*
Go down Atherley Road towards the sea. Turn right at the Mayfair Hotel to follow the walk above the sea on your left. This is Eastcliff Promenade.

3 *Turn right up Delphi Road, walking with the sea on your right and past Channel View Hotel on your left. Go ahead along the cliff walk.*

2 *Reach the Cliff Lift on your left. Either take it down to the remains of the pier or go ahead 100 yards (90 m) and turn left down the path and long flight of steps to reach the remains of the pier. Facing the pier, go left along Shanklin Esplanade. Bend left with the road at its end to climb back to Hope Road.*

Over

A The Cliff Lift was built in 1956 as a replacement for the 1891 version that rendered such sterling services during the invasion of Normandy in June 1944. A complex system of pumps and pipelines from here formed PLUTO (Pipeline Under The Ocean) to supply the invasion forces with fuel, and the lift was used during its construction.

B Out to sea, over Sandown Bay, is the site of the loss of *HMS Eurydice*. The tragedy happened on the afternoon of Sunday, 22nd March, 1878. Simultaneously, in Windsor, Sir John MacNiell told the Bishop of Ripon that he had just had a vision of a ship under full sail with her gunports imprudently open, despite a mighty black squall about to envelop her. This was indeed the case. The actual events were witnessed by a small boy named Winston Churchill. The 921 ton frigate sailed into a thick, driving blizzard with all her 26 gunports open. This caused *HMS Eurydice*, a training ship launched in 1843, made obsolete then recommissioned, to capsize. She was on her way back from a tour of the West Indies with 366 men aboard. Only two survived. One of them said that the whole crew, officers and men, had all been drunk at the time, celebrating their homecoming. Sir Winston Churchill was to note in *My Early Life* how the story of divers on the wreck finding corpses eaten by fish was to leave a scar on his mind.

C Sandown pier has all the usual attractions plus sea cruises.

D Christ Church graveyard contains graves of those drowned when *HMS Eurydice* went down.

E Whilst in Sandown, you could visit the Geology Museum at the corner of High Street and Victoria Road (in the same building as the library). Its extensive collection of fossils and rocks is rich in local finds, including the recently excavated dinosaur fossils. It is open Mon – Sat 9.30am – 5pm, and admission is free. There is an excellent youth hostel in Fitzroy Street.

Sandown

SHANKLIN CHINE

4.5 miles (7.2 km) Moderate

0   1 mile
0   1 km

There is no need to wander far from a major resort to enjoy the peace and quiet of country footpaths, as this walk near Shanklin illustrates. Although there is a steep climb to a ridge, the views over Shanklin and Sandown Bay are well worth the effort. The walk starts at Shanklin's British Rail station, the terminus of the line from Ryde Pier Head. Built in 1866, it now uses ex-London Transport Underground trains. This walk can be linked with Walk **35** at point **1**.

1 *Start from Shanklin's British Rail station, on the line from Ryde. There is a car park here. If you arrive at the bus station, walk along Languard Road, turn right into Marine Crossroad and then left into Regent Street to reach the start of the walk.*

Go right along the path behind the car park sign and down steps to Landguard Road. Turn right, then fork left down a signposted bridle road to America Wood.

2 *Go through a holiday village, bearing right towards Scotchells (path SS18). Go ahead at the next signpost along path SS17. Continue to a crosstracks. Turn left along the signposted bridle road 18A to Ninham Farm and America Wood.*

3 *At the entrance to Ninham campsite, turn right along the lane towards Willow Brook. Go through a gate and go left along a bridleway towards America Wood.* **Do not** *be tempted by a path on your right.*

4 *Go ahead along bridleway 19 to America Wood, bearing left to a gate in the fence. Enter the wood and bear left on a path to reach America Cottages, where there are tea gardens.*

5 *Turn right along a waymarked path into the woods. Turn left at the next waymark post and follow blue arrows to emerge at a road. Cross this (the A3020) carefully, go right for 10 yards (9 m), then turn left past houses to a stile ahead. Cross the old railway line and continue over a stile along the signposted path NC39 to Shanklin Down.*

6 *Ignore a footbridge and stile on your left. Pass another stile on your right but go over a stile ahead and another stile in the next field corner. Continue up steep steps through trees to a stile in the fence at the top. Cross this into a field and turn left to follow a hedge on your left. Continue over a stile along the signposted path SS10 to Shanklin, ignoring a path to your right. Walk ahead to a stile beside a gate.*

7 *Descend over stiles and as waymarked to reach the A3055 near a church. Go right then left along path 91 to Priory Road. Go ahead up Popham Road.*

8 *Bear left just before Rylstone Gardens. Pass Shanklin Chine on your right and turn left to the A3055. Go right along the pavement, then left up Languard Road to return to the station.*

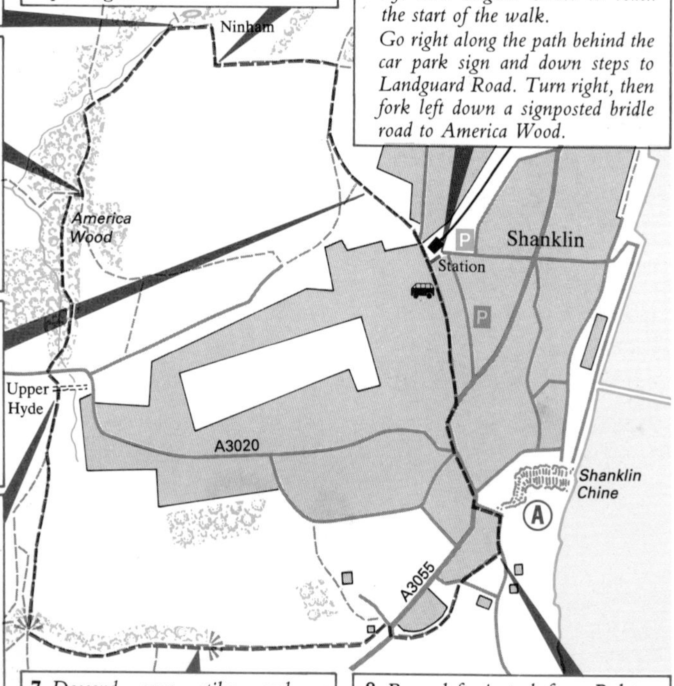

A Shanklin Chine is open Apr - Oct daily 9.30am - 5.30pm (10pm Jun - Aug) and is floodlit after dusk. Admission charge.

Map labels: Ninham, America Wood, Upper Hyde, A3020, A3055, Shanklin, Station, Shanklin Chine, (A)

LUCCOMBE CHINE

3 miles (4.8 km) Strenuous

This walk involves a strenuous climb almost to the very top of the highest point of the island, the 787 foot (240 m) summit of St. Boniface Down, from where there are splendid views. By contrast, the walk then descends to follow a woodland path through The Landslip before following a smugglers' path right down to the beach at Luccombe Chine.

1 Start from the Nansen Hill (The Landslip) car park on the seaward side of the A3055 just north of Bonchurch. Bus nos 16 & 17 (Ryde to Ventnor) stop here. Cross the road with care and go ahead over a gate on your left and a bus stop on your right. Go uphill along a path to cross a stile and bear left uphill to a signpost before a radar station.

2 Go left from the signpost downhill along path V42 towards Bonchurch. Cross a stile ahead and descend with the sea in front of you. Reach bushes but do not go ahead down steps to a stile. Instead, turn left to follow a path along the foot of the grassy downland above bushes on your right. Pass the last house on your right, then turn right down to the road (and not ahead over a stile into woodland). Cross the A3055 carefully and turn left along the pavement.

7 Go ahead over a lane and up path 6, to the right of cottages. Climb steps to the road and turn left back to the start of the walk.

3 Turn right into the Smuggler's Haven Tea Gardens. With your back to the café and with a lawn in front of you, descend to the bottom right corner of the lawn where there are steps. Go down these, passing an old shelter on your left. Go right beside a wall (and the sea) on your left. Descend steps through the Devil's Chimney (a cleft in a rock) and continue down

6 Retrace your steps to the path junction, go left for 10 yards (9 m) and turn right up a lane for 50 yards (45 m). Then go right on a waymarked path to Luccombe Farm. Turn left along path 5 to Bonchurch.

5 Fork right at a track junction to pass Dunnose Cottage on your left. Leave the track at a bend to take a path ahead for 10 yards (9 m), then turn right down to Luccombe Chine. Go down to a beach.

4 Turn left along the signposted path V65A to Luccombe. This attractive woodland path passes a wishing seat (a marked rock) on your left. Continue ahead along a walled path (leading to Smuggler's Cottage) to reach Rosecliff Lodge on your right. Bear left along a track but pass the signposted path to the main road and the bus stops on your left.

steps through trees. Ignore side paths and go down steps along a waymarked path to a signpost near a lower shelter, on your right.

A In tradition St. Boniface came from Devon, was trained in a monastery in Hampshire and came to this area to preach in the eighth century. The down that bears his name is the highest point on the island, although the actual summit is within the radar station.

B The Landslip is a picturesque jungle based on unstable foundations, as was shown in 1810, and again in 1928, when it all slipped. There is a bed of gault clay underlying the chalk and upper greensand which slopes towards the shore and slips downwards after wet weather. Hydrangeas turn the place pink in summer.

C Smugglers used to run up the 200 plus steps of Luccombe Chine in the dark carrying brandy barrels and risking capture by the Revenue men. Subsidence caused cottagers living at the foot of the Chine to move out in the 1890s. Giant dinosaur bones were found on the beach here in 1946.

ST. HELENS

6 miles (9.7 km) Easy

There is plenty of variety on this route, from a prime site for wild flowers to the attractive streets and yachting atmosphere of Seaview. The countryside inland is pleasant, and the sea wall provides views across to the mainland, or of ships in the Channel. You could even have a ghostly encounter on your path as you pass a farm once worked by monks from Nettlestone priory, the church tower of which is now a landmark for mariners.

A St. Helens has a large village green. Half-way along Upper Green Road is where Sophie Dawes was born in 1792. She was the daughter of a local smuggler, Dicky Dawes. He died when Sophie was young and the family were forced to enter the House of Industry at Parkhurst. At the age of 13, Sophie was sent to work for a local farmer. Two years later, she left him for the big, wide world. First stop was Portsmouth, where Sophie worked as a chambermaid at the George Hotel. From there she made it to London where she worked as an assistant in a milliner's shop. Sacked after an affair with a water-carrier, she sold oranges in Covent Garden and later found work in a brothel. There she met the servant of the exiled Duc de Bourbon, who recommended her to his master. The 52 year-old duke was the last of the Condés and the heir to their fortune. Sophie and the duke got on so well together that she was settled in a house in Bloomsbury with £800 per annum by 1812. Her lover also paid for her education. The duke rushed home to France at the restoration of 1814, but Sophie resolved not to let go of him. She followed and kept reminding the duke that only she really understood his problems. Upon the death of his father in 1818, the duke became a fabulously rich man. Sophie rushed to console him, but to maintain outward appearances, Sophie pretended to be the prince's illegitimate daughter, as she was married at the time to a Monsieur de Fouchères, an officer in King Louis XVIII's Guards, and not a possessive man. The couple came to live in the Palais Bourbon, where the husband was given a job in the household and Sophie had the privileges of a 'daughter'. Only the king's court was barred to her. Having 'arrived', the smuggler's daughter began to show her coarse side, frightening the 60 year-old prince. She dominated him and his entire household. The prince's hairdresser became her lover, while her nephew, James Dawes, was brought from London to be the prince's first equerry. Next, her mother was brought from St. Helens to comfortable lodgings in Paris and Mary Anne, Sophie's elder sister, was married to a Captain-Adjutant-Major and set up house in Paris with a dowry of 100,000 francs from the prince.

The bubble burst when Sophie's husband found out that she was really the prince's mistress, not his daughter, and divorced her. Aware of her vulnerability, Sophie then began an association with the Duke of Orléans (the future King Louis Philippe) and managed to manipulate this relationship for her own financial and material gain. Thinking perhaps that her luck was now running out, Sophie wisely turned her assets into cash and went on a grand tour of Europe before returning to England, buying a mansion near Christchurch and a house in Hyde Park Square. With time now to reflect upon her sins, Sophie found religion. Her 90 year-old mother was brought back to die in a convent in Hammersmith, and most of her huge fortune was given to charity. Sophie died of a heart attack in 1840.

B Seaview's Flamingo Park is open Apr daily 2 - 5.30pm, May - Sept daily 10am - 5.30pm, Oct daily 2 - 5pm. Admission charge.

C Now a hotel, Nettlestone Priory was once a farm for St. Helens' Priory. It is reputedly haunted by a ghostly Blue Lady whose stuffed dog (now over 200 years old) still hangs at the top of the stairs.

D There was a Cluniac priory here in 1090, but it was suppressed in 1414 (for being French). The old St. Helen's church was ruined by the sea in 1720.

Over

0   1 mile

0   1 km

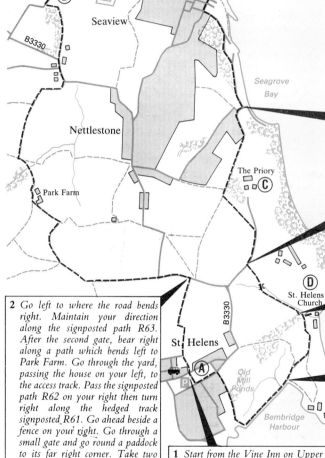

3 Go right beside the road till it bends, then take the sea wall ahead.

4 Rejoin the road at Hayward House and bear left along the Esplanade. Go inland up Seaview's High Street to Pier Road, the third on your left. Turn left along it, go right at a fork and continue along a path to emerge at a Coastal Path signpost on Fernclose Road.

5 Bear right up Fernclose Road, which deteriorates into a track. Pass The Priory on your left, then a stone cottage, before bearing left along an enclosed path. Reach an access lane and go right, passing a Holiday Centre on your left.

6 Turn left through a kissing-gate to follow path R85 down to a footbridge and stile at the foot of the field. Cross these and go left along the edge of the field to a stile in the corner. Go over this to a lane.

7 Go left, ignoring the access road to a car park on your right. Reach the ruins of St. Helens Church, then turn back to the access road to the car park. Go left along it until level with the National Trust car park. Bear right along a faint path to the old Mill Dam wall.

8 Go ahead along the Dam wall, then turn right up Mill Road. Reach St. Helens' Green and go left along Lower Green Road before bearing right across the green to Upper Green Road and the Vine Inn.

2 Go left to where the road bends right. Maintain your direction along the signposted path R63. After the second gate, bear right along a path which bends left to Park Farm. Go through the yard, passing the house on your left, to the access track. Pass the signposted path R62 on your right then turn right along the hedged track signposted R61. Go ahead beside a fence on your right. Go through a small gate and go round a paddock to its far right corner. Take two gates to reach an access track. Bear right to the B3330 road. Go left to the Wishing Well pub. Turn right along the track which passes the front of the pub. This continues as

1 Start from the Vine Inn on Upper Green Road, St. Helens. The no 8 bus (Newport to Ryde) stops here.

a narrow path to a road. Go right to the sea-front.

Cars can be parked at the roadside nearby.
Take a path to the right of the inn. Ignore a path on your left but follow a hedged path to the B3330 road.

Walk 39
BEMBRIDGE
5 miles (8 km) Easy

This is an easy walk around the island's most fashionable resort. Prince Charles and Princess Anne came to play on the beach here when they were children. The druids used to meet here, until the Roman legions landed on the local beaches in AD43. Nelson often anchored his fleet offshore in the late 18th century, waiting for a fair wind and training his crew where they couldn't escape. The locals lived in fear of the press-gang.

A The Maritime Museum at Bembridge is well worth a visit. This is the creation of a local professional diver and displays many artefacts found on the numerous shipwrecks around the coast of the island. These include Spanish 'pieces of eight'. There is also an interesting display of diving equipment and a large display giving an impression of what it's like to be a diver working on an old sailing shipwreck. Models of ships and a display on the history of the Bembridge Lifeboat fill other galleries. If you have children with you, don't forget to show them the 'merman', actually a Victorian trick made by combining the top of a monkey with the bottom of a fish. It brought in the pennies at fairs. The museum is open Easter – Oct daily 10am – 5.30pm. Admission charge.

B A well here was famous for its water, which was said to keep fresh on voyages around the world. The Navy regularly drew from it before setting sail.

C Bembridge Lifeboat Station is open to public view on certain days. The inshore lifeboat station was where Bembridge's first lifeboats were housed. The Bembridge lifeboat *Queen Victoria* rescued the crew of the naval torpedo boat 059 when it ran aground on Bembridge Ledge in December 1899. On board was Commander Beatty, who went on to become an admiral, and lead the battle-cruiser squadron at the biggest naval battle in history, the Battle of Jutland, in 1916. He received the surrender of the German fleet in 1918.

D Bembridge School houses the largest single collection of the work of John Ruskin, the social reformer. Visits by appointment only.

E Bembridge Windmill is in the care of the National Trust, and is open Apr – Nov Sun – Fri, and Sat Jul – Aug 10am – 5pm. Admission charge.

Bembridge Windmill

Over

2 Turn right up the track opposite the Pilot Boat Inn along the signposted Coastal Path. Reach a junction and go left. Then, just before the sea, turn right along path BB6.

3 Follow the path through trees and down to a shingle bank. Follow this, with the sea on your left, to the sea wall, which will lead you to the Lifeboat Station.

1 Start from the Maritime Museum in the centre of Bembridge, on your right as you take the B3395 (Sherborne Street) towards St. Helens. The no 8 bus (Shanklin to Ryde) stops here, and cars can be parked with consideration nearby (or park at the car park near the Lifeboat Station and start from point **4**).
With your back to the museum, turn right down to the harbour.

9 Continue to the High Street and go ahead until Sherborne Street and the Maritime Museum are on your left.

8 Turn right at a junction to follow a bridleway uphill to a windmill, on your left.

7 Go left for 100 yards (90 m) and turn right along a path which passes a campsite on your left. Go ahead through woodland, across a road and along another woodland path.

6 Turn right, away from the Coastal Path. Reach the drive of Bembridge School and bear left along the footpath through the trees to a road.

5 Keep to the top of the cliffs along the Coastal Path, which is well-maintained with stiles, footbridges and signposts. Continue to the far end of Bembridge School playing-fields on your right.

4 From the Lifeboat Station car park, continue with the sea on your left across an area of grass. Turn right up a narrow path, then go left along the signposted Coastal Path. Go right at Forelands Farm, pass Paddock Drive and turn left to follow Beachfield Road to its end. Turn right past the Coastguard Lookout, cross the car park of the Crab & Lobster Inn and take the path on your left, close to the cliffs. Follow the Coastal path.

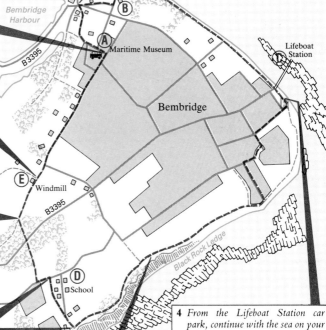

Walk 40
RED CLIFF
4 miles (6.4 km) Moderate

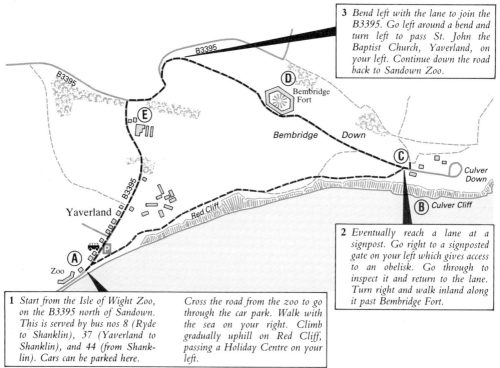

0 | | | | | 1 mile
0 | | | | 1 km

Magnificent Culver Cliff is the pride of Sandown Bay. This walk takes you along the Coastal Path up to the monument at the top.

The Red Cliff which you climb is composed of Wealdon Clay and the bones of dinosaurs have been exposed here. Culver Down is

made of the more resilient chalk which runs the length of the island from the Needles. There is a café on Culver Cliff, and fine views.

3 *Bend left with the lane to join the B3395. Go left around a bend and turn left to pass St. John the Baptist Church, Yaverland, on your left. Continue down the road back to Sandown Zoo.*

2 *Eventually reach a lane at a signpost. Go right to a signposted gate on your left which gives access to an obelisk. Go through to inspect it and return to the lane. Turn right and walk inland along it past Bembridge Fort.*

1 *Start from the Isle of Wight Zoo, on the B3395 north of Sandown. This is served by bus nos 8 (Ryde to Shanklin), 37 (Yaverland to Shanklin), and 44 (from Shanklin). Cars can be parked here.*

Cross the road from the zoo to go through the car park. Walk with the sea on your right. Climb gradually uphill on Red Cliff, passing a Holiday Centre on your left.

A Sandown Zoo is housed in one of Palmerston's forts, completed in 1866 as a link in the chain of defences against a feared French invasion. Its finest hours were during World War II when it duplicated Shanklin Lift as a pumping station for PLUTO (the Pipeline Under The Ocean). Its seemingly indestructible granite walls now keep the animals in.

B Culver Cliffs rise dramatically from the sea. It was at their foot that the tug *Harry Sherman* came to grief in October 1970, after it had taken part in the rescue of the blazing oil tanker *Pacific Glory*.

C This obelisk is a memorial to the first Earl of Yarborough (Charles Pelham), the founder of the Royal Yacht Squadron.

D Bembridge Fort was constructed between 1862 and 1867 by Lord Palmerston's government.

E The church of St. John the Baptist, Yaverland, is of Norman origin.

62